Rereading Fluency

Process, Practice, and Policy

Bess Altwerger
Nancy Jordan
Nancy Rankie Shelton

Foreword by Richard L. Allington

HEINEMANN
Portsmouth, NH

Heinemann
361 Hanover Street
Portsmouth, NH 03801–3912
www.heinemann.com

Offices and agents throughout the world

Library of Congress Cataloging-in-Publication Data
Altwerger, Bess.
    Rereading fluency : process, practice, and policy / Bess Altwerger, Nancy Jordan, Nancy Rankie Shelton ; foreword by Richard L. Allington.
        p. cm.
    Includes bibliographical references and index.
    ISBN-13: 978-0-325-01034-2
    ISBN-10: 0-325-01034-X
    1. Reading comprehension. 2. Fluency (Language learning).   I. Jordan, Nancy C.   II. Shelton, Nancy Rankie.   III. Title.

LB1050.45.A45 2007
428.4'3—dc22   2007025644

Editor: Leigh Peake
Production management: Appingo
Production coordination: Vicki Kasabian
Cover design: Night & Day Design
Typesetter: Appingo
Manufacturing: Louise Richardson

Printed in the United States of America on acid-free paper
11 10 09 08   VP   2 3 4 5

Dedicated to the teachers and students who
struggle each day to find meaning, purpose, and joy in literacy
learning despite the many challenges that have been
placed in their way. They are our heroes.

Contents

Part III: RETHINKING FLUENCY

Foreword

Rereading Fluency: Process, Practice, and Policy is an important and timely book. It is important because the authors present a number of challenges to the dominant model of reading instruction and development—challenges raised from the analyses of the data they gathered in schools and classrooms.

Their challenges are far from the only ones raised about the dominant paradigm. The data-based findings presented here are reinforced by a variety of studies already available. But most of these studies attended to only a single challenge to the current implementation of "evidence-based" reading instruction. Altwerger, Jordan, and Shelton take a broader view.

Nonetheless, let me note just a few of the studies that provide good evidence, converging evidence, that the challenges presented in this book need serious consideration from teachers, administrators, and policy makers.

Challenge: Good readers are fast readers. Walczyk and Griffith-Ross (2007), Pressley (2006), and Buly and Valencia (2002) argue that this simply is not true. Walczyk and Griffith-Ross report that "slowing down" is the most commonly used strategy when readers encounter difficulty. The second strategy is rereading. Both result in slower reading rates. Both result in better comprehension. Pressley found that "children can often read with great speed and accuracy and yet recall few of the ideas in the text they read" (2006, 209). In a similar vein, Buly and Valencia found that nearly 20 percent of their struggling readers could read fast and accurately but exhibit almost no recall or understanding of what they read. While focusing instruction on reading faster may generate observed gains on rate/fluency measures, such gains do not indicate that children are improving as readers.

Challenge: Reading rate and accuracy measures can be used to develop better instruction. Schilling and others (2007) found that 37 percent of the third-grade students who were identified as at low risk on the DIBELS oral reading fluency assessment fell below grade level reading achievement on the Iowa Test of Basic Skills administered at the end of the school year. Because their DIBELS benchmark scores indicated little or no risk of reading failure, many of these students were denied access to instruction that might have resolved the risk that wasn't evident on the DIBELS tests.

Challenge: Commercial core reading programs will improve reading achievement. In a large-scale analysis across thirty-seven school districts, McGill-Franzen and others (2006) found that in schools that used one of the state-approved commercial core reading programs to guide instruction, one-third of the third-grade students, on average, failed to achieve the minimum benchmark on the state reading assessment. In all these schools the DIBELS assessment was also being used to inform instruction. But still large numbers of children failed to learn to read. So much for the science of fluency assessment and core reading program requirements.

I could go on, but I hope that I have made my point: The findings reported in *Rereading Fluency: Process, Practice, and Policy* are supported by other scientific research. It is the scope of the work reported in this book that sets it apart. Additionally, the authors do not just criticize current policies and practices but offer alternatives for improving the quality of reading assessment and instruction.

This book challenges the conventional view of how to improve reading instruction and achievement. It is through such challenges that science ultimately finds its way to fact.

Richard L. Allington, Ph.D.
University of Tennessee

References

Buly, M. R., and S. W. Valencia. 2002. "Below the Bar: Profiles of Students Who Fail State Reading Assessments." *Educational Evaluation and Policy Analysis* 24 (3): 219–39.

McGill-Franzen, A., C. Zmach, K. Solic, and J. L. Zeig. 2006. "The Confluence of Two Policy Mandates: Core Reading Programs and Third-Grade Retention in Florida." *Elementary School Journal* 107 (1): 67–91.

Pressley, M. P. 2006. *Reading Instruction That Works*, 3d ed. New York: Guilford.

Schilling, S. G., J. F.Carlisle, S. E. Scott, and J. Zeng. 2007. "Are Fluency Measures Accurate Predictors of Reading Achievement?" *Elementary School Journal* 107 (5): 429–48.

Walczyk, J. A., and D. A. Griffith-Ross. 2007. "How Important Is Reading Skill Fluency for Comprehension?" *Reading Teacher* 60 (6): 560–69.

Acknowledgments

We are profoundly grateful to our past and present Towson University colleagues—Poonam Arya, Deb Lang, Barbara Laster, Lijin Jin, Prisca Martens, Pat Wilson, and Nancy Wiltz—whose participation in data collection and analysis for our original study made this book possible. We also want to express our gratitude to Lois Bridges who embraced this project in its early stages and Leigh Peake at Heinemann for her patient and encouraging support through its completion.

Bess Altwerger

Writing this book would not have been possible for me without the inspirational leadership and courage of colleagues and friends whose voices of opposition and resistance to repressive literacy policies would not be silenced. First and foremost among these are my mentors and lifelong friends, Kenneth and Yetta Goodman, who have shown us all how to face overwhelming adversity with dignity, intellectual rigor, and abiding kindness. My dear "sister," Barbara Flores, has kept her heart and mind steadfastly focused on the rights of all children to an education that values and celebrates their cultures and languages. She rejuvenates my spirit on a regular basis. My soulmate, Carole Edelsky, has continued to challenge me with her profound theoretical insights and political analyses, despite the "McCarthyism" of our times. Her wit and humor has often kept me laughing instead of crying!

So many others have inspired me with the truth and passion of their written and spoken words. Though I am honored to know some of them personally, I consider myself a student of them all. Among these brave and brilliant teachers are Dick Allington, Gerry Bracey, Linda Christiansen, Gerry Coles, Elaine Garan, Elizabeth Jaeger, Steve Krashen, Donaldo Macedo, Susan Ohanian, Denny Taylor, and Joanne Yatvin.

I am forever grateful to Dorothy Menosky, my first real mentor and professional mom, who set me on the path to Arizona and my entire professional future with her bewildering belief in me and a few swift kicks in just the right place.

Finally, I owe my greatest gratitude to my family for their unfailing love and support. My children, Erika and Asher, have grown into adults with the critical intellect and loving kindness that fills me with hope for the future. My loving husband, Steven Strauss, encouraged and supported me throughout this project as he has throughout my entire career. His passion for justice and optimism for humanity continues to inspire me every day of my life.

Nancy Jordan

I would like to thank the many teachers, students, and administrators that I learned from and with during my eighteen years working for Fairfax County Public Schools in Virginia. Particularly, I would like to recognize Bess Osborn for taking a chance when she hired me, a rookie, as a Title I Language Arts teacher; Edwin Grady III, principal, who supported so many professional growth opportunities for me as a reading teacher; Gloria McDonald who, as she was helping me write a teacher-researcher grant proposal, confidently said, "Someday, I will be able to say I knew her when" (Gloria, I never thought that I would tri-author a book); Ann McCallum and Bev Morrison whose mentoring opened the doors that ushered in my interest in teacher research; and Corrine Rogers and Jean Frey, fellow teacher researchers, who were there with their spirited conversations when I took my first steps into research. In addition, I would like to thank Angela Jaggar, John Mayher, and Gordon Pradl, my dissertation committee at New York University, for always challenging my thinking, believing in my work, and contributing to my learning. I would also like to thank Darlene Forest, a fellow doctoral student and friend, for her advice and support throughout the years.

This book would not have been possible if my family, daughter Michel and partner David, had not left me to work, cooked, and cleaned, and basically fended for themselves. Their love and encouragement sustained me during the research and the writing of this book. And finally, a heartfelt appreciation goes to my colleagues Bess and Nancy for their knowledge, hard work, and friendship and for such a brilliant collaboration.

Nancy Shelton

My life has taken many twists and turns on its way to writing this book. Throughout my journey, one thing has remained constant: I have been surrounded by people who have encouraged me to keep focused not on what is, but on what can be. During my ten years as a public school teacher in Alachua County, I taught side-by-side with the most educated, talented faculty in the state of Florida. Four of those wonderful teachers influenced me in ways that only other teachers can understand—laughing and crying, agreeing and disagreeing, working and playing, teaching and learning while meeting the demands of teaching. Lou Merrill, Gloria Jean Merriex, Cassie Lisa Jacobs, and Donna Sides—you are special teachers who pushed me to be the best I could be for every single student who entered my classroom.

I could not have made the tough transition from the elementary classroom to the university classroom without the dedicated support of my doctoral committee at the University of Florida (UF). While working for my Masters in Education I was lucky enough to take a language arts class with Linda Lamme. Long after I completed my coursework at UF, Linda supported me in every effort, listening to long hours of a teacher rambling about her students and sharing conversations about great works of children's literature. Before long, Danling Fu joined the faculty, and my ties to UF strengthened. Danling's knowledge of children's writing and her interest in helping teachers create authentic writing environments drew me into a friendship and collaboration that inspired me to reenroll as a student. Danling taught me how to listen, how to see children as writers, and how to find positive meaning in every task set before me. During my doctoral journey at UF I met Dick Allington, but in reality I knew him long before that—his book *No Quick Fix* served as my guidebook in my early years of teaching. I could not have survived without it! His strong voice for teachers was and continues to be one of the greatest examples of professional voice in the United States. And James McLeskey helped me find the researcher deep within my teaching, honoring both what I emerged from and what I would become.

There are others who have accompanied me on this great educational expedition—too many to name but I would be remiss if I didn't single out a few: my wonderful colleagues at UMBC who have made me feel at home in one short semester; Morna McNulty, Bess Altwerger, Greg Bryant, Nechie King, LiJun Jin, Pam Morgan, Dave Volke, and Prisca Martens who helped me adjust to life as an assistant professor at Towson University; Betsy McClure who has been my friend since we met at SUNY Albany in 1975; Xenia Hadjioannou, my academic sister who was at my side through all the stress of doctoral work; my sisters Jeanne So and Carol Waller who have always helped me find strength when I was at my weakest points; my parents C. Jane and Charles Rankie who were my first and most loyal teachers; and most especially my husband Jack and son Conrad, without whom life would have little meaning.

To all of you I owe a profound debt of gratitude.

Why Do We Need a Critical Look at Fluency?

Matthew Bruun of the *Massachusetts Telegram* brags:

> Based on indicators such as national test scores and graduation rates, Massachusetts was ranked first in the country for student achievement in kindergarten through Grade 12.

The news can't always be this good. Terry Organ was handed the dismal task of reporting:

> Arizona finds itself in familiar territory … near the bottom in education. (*Kingman* [Ariz.] *Daily Miner* 2007)

Newspaper headlines all over the nation call constant attention to education. It has become common practice to publicly compare schools at the state, district, and school levels. We now routinely publish standardized test scores in local newspapers.

While this media frenzy may have been rooted in a genuine concern for the state of public education, it nevertheless has had many negative consequences. Teachers in classrooms across the country are under the microscope, subject to the prejudicial opinions of those with little understanding of the real life complexities of teaching. Furthermore, journalists have become the voice of authority regarding instruction and assessment, marginalizing the value of educational research. A headline like this screams a warning message to the community: New Study Finds More Than $1 Billion in Public Funds to Improve Schools Yielded Little Student Academic Improvement (*Earthtimes* Jan 16 2007). Trust in our schools and our teachers are continually challenged by such alarming messages.

In recent years, differences in theoretical positions in regard to teaching and learning have moved away from the professional community of educators and educational researchers. This shift has been heavily supported by conservative think-tanks, representatives of publishing companies, and politicians (Allington 2002; Altwerger 2005; Garan 2001; Coles 2003; Poyner and Wolfe 2005). As a result, important educational decisions are being made around corporate roundtables rather than in faculty meetings. Nowhere has this been felt more than in early literacy education. More attention is lavished on reading than any other content area. Federal and state legislation mandating Adequate Yearly Progress (AYP) in reading threatens to use legislation to take control of schools away from educators and place it under the control of politicians and entrepreneurs.

Though the reading wars have been fought for generations, the new attack has all but silenced views that are not supported by the federal government. The focus placed on improving reading performance nationwide holds the singular notion that testing is the key to increasing performance of students and teachers. With this view dominating the federal scene, decisions on how to improve academic performance of students have become a cry for school reform that equate to increased testing. Pressure is being placed on educators to use "proven programs" to increase reading performance of students, federal and state funding is being limited to schools that implement "proven programs," and voucher systems are gaining support throughout the nation as viable alternatives to free, public education.

The current efforts to control teaching through testing has created "a constant battle for the control of classrooms between educational programmers and testers who want to hold teachers accountable for delivering instruction in the misguided manner they think children are best taught, and teachers who know there is a better way" (Smith 1986, 195–196). According to Smith, forcing teachers into programmatic instruction is not new to education. It is a symptom of the all too disturbing fact that "the unspoken assumption behind the production and promotion of all programmatic instruction is that someone outside the classroom can make better decisions than the teacher in the classroom" (Smith 1986, 125). Forced change in reading education, in the form of adherence to mandated assessment programs as well as commercial reading instruction programs, has hijacked the minds and methodologies of teachers. And the media have provided the ammunition by keeping the focus of the public on so-called failing schools.

The media has failed to report research that shows how mandating instructional approaches marginalizes professional educators (Ford 2001), is in direct contrast to what we know about the need for teachers to hold beliefs that support their methodology (Shelton 2005), and recognizes the power of the teachers' professional knowledge (Giroux 1992; Short and Burke 1996; Sleeter 1996). Scandals are buried more than they are exposed in the press. Consider the overwhelming lack of attention given to the Inspector General's Final Inspection Report of the Reading First Program's Grant Application Process (ED-OIG/113-F0017) until months after its release when finally in Spring 2007 the House Committee on Education and the Workforce held hearings on the matter. Both the report and the hearings unveiled the intentional and deliberate conflicts of interest of Reading First officials and consultants who approved Reading First federal grants. When there is limited media coverage disclosing the cronyism that costs taxpayers billions of dollars and causes students to be placed in rigid, stifling reading programs, teachers have no social capital or professional energy to fight back.

Educators most often have the best interest of the students in mind when making curriculum decisions, but administrators are often influenced by public policy, which is directly influenced by public opinion and public law. The policy making process is shaped by countless people and social forces (Lindblom and Woodhouse 1993). This is problematic because "the mind at its best simply cannot grasp the complexity of social reality" (5). Yet teachers are expected to balance the social and practical realities of curriculum reform.

Reading Wars

Reading education and policy struggles in the United States today are a continuation of the historic struggles and conflicts amongst the multiple perspectives grounding our reading curricula. The ongoing disagreement about how teachers should teach reading and the continued struggle to accommodate diverse learners creates tension.

Disagreement about how language is learned and opposing views of what constitutes knowledge precipitated the struggle between conflicting traditions in the reading curriculum. As far back as 1895, opposing views of language curriculum were evident in "The Report of the Sub-committee on the Correlation of Studies in Elementary Education," which became known as the "Committee of Fifteen" (1895). While the committee introduced the "Language Studies" discussion stating "there is first to be noted the prominent place of language study that takes the form of reading, penmanship, and grammar in the first eight years' work of the school" (44), the committee also recognized that "the most practical knowledge of all, it will be admitted, is a knowledge of human nature—a knowledge that enables one to combine with his fellow-men and to share with them the physical and spiritual wealth of the race" (47). And so the debates in reading curriculum were staged. On one side is a behaviorist perspective of learning as well as the theories of formalism, positivism, and the scientific movement; on the other side is a constructivist perspective of learning and progressive educational thought evolving from the work of Dewey.

The struggle between reading instruction traditions has been most recently complicated by all of the following: the passage of the Reading Excellence Act (REA), the National Institute of Child Health and Human Development's (NICHD) release of the National Reading Panel Summary (1999), and the passage of No Child Left Behind (NCLB) legislation. All of these promote phonics as the most important component in early reading development. The REA redefined reading and attached all REA funding to mandatory use of its definition. The National Reading Panel Summary has refocused the emphasis of reading instruction on discrete skills as the critical foundation needed for reading development and calls for the immediate application of this in classrooms nationwide. The Department of Education, under the Reading First initiative of NCLB, has endorsed assessment programs that treat reading as a collection of discrete, quantitatively measurable skills and packaged reading programs that promote systematic skill instruction focusing primarily on phonics. This trend has resulted in drawing on oral reading for almost all early reading assessment, as well as making oral reading fluency a focus of instruction.

As a result, teachers are being directed to devote a large portion of their instructional time to improving oral reading. But should oral reading have this prominent role in elementary classrooms? Many teachers are mandated to use commercially produced fluency assessment instruments to measure students' reading speed and accuracy of anything from letters and nonsense words to short passages. As speed and accuracy in oral reading, rather than quality and substance of reading for meaning, increasingly determines students' literacy futures in school, it is important to examine oral reading from a historical perspective.

Historical Overview of Oral Reading

Historically, oral reading was the only reading practiced in Western cultures and the only form of reading taught in school (Allington 1983). The dominance of oral reading continued unchallenged until 1880 when the role of silent reading began to emerge and an "oral versus silent reading debate" (Allington 1983, 829) began. According to Allington, three schools of thought developed regarding oral reading:

> The first, and perhaps the most prevalent, depicted oral reading as a means to an ultimate end—proficient silent reading. The second held that oral reading was a detriment to the ultimate end—proficient silent reading. Finally, a third school held that oral reading was not a tool, as such, but rather an art form whose techniques were worth mastering. (1983, 830)

During the following years, instructional practices fell in and out of favor as oral and non-oral instruction and various ways to evaluate oral reading developed. Quantifying errors in reading provided the predominant means of measuring successful efforts until the mid-1960s when Goodman's research (1967) shifted the focus of oral reading to miscues. For the first time, the quality of inaccuracies became an important part of the evaluation of oral reading performance.

In Goodman's miscue analysis procedure, the effect of miscues on meaning during reading replaced the quantifying of errors as the most significant information to gather about readers. *Qualitative* analysis of oral reading reflects a student's processing and comprehending of the text being read. The *quantitative* perspective of oral reading drives the body of fluency research that links measures of rate and accuracy to comprehension scores on standardized tests (Shinn et al. 1992; Good and Kaminski 2002).

Regardless of whether their theoretical perspective is quantitative or qualitative, many teachers have always had an intuitive sense that the fluency or fluidity of oral reading is an indicator of successful reading. But recently, oral reading fluency, specifically reading rate and accuracy, has assumed a lead role in literacy curriculum and assessment. In the 1990s, prior to the current era of accountability, teachers made decisions about what text to use as their assessment, what benchmarks to use for their students, and how often to formally monitor oral reading progress. Oral reading was used as a tool to help identify instructional strategies that would help develop a reader's comprehension. It was not considered to be the sole indicator of a student's reading proficiency, but a single factor that provided useful information. Silent reading comprehension stood out as the most important concern.

Currently, fluency instruction and assessment have become priorities in national literacy policy, and silent reading has taken a back seat to oral reading. Leading Reading First proponents have supported instructional assessment of discrete skills such as letter naming, phonemic segmentation, and proficiency in reading nonsense words, ignoring the importance of comprehension until young readers master these decontextualized skills. Incorrectly citing the National Reading Panel report, several advocates of "scientific programs," including the past president of the International Reading Association (IRA) Timothy Shanahan, downplay the importance of self-selected silent reading, professing it has no place in the school curriculum. When challenged by several prominent reading researchers, Shanahan defended himself in his first presidential column in *Reading Today*, the IRA's news publication, stating "sustained silent reading (SSR) is probably not such a good idea."(Shanahan 2006, 12)

Symptoms of this narrow-minded approach to reading are being felt in classrooms across the nation. Teachers are forced to assess and instruct students using materials and programs they believe limit their students' reading development. Lisa Jacobs explains the problem well when she describes her third-grade students:

They think good reading is reading as fast as you can. Sometimes I have to say 'Whoa, whoa, whoa, whoa! There's a period there. Go back and reread that.' Or they put inflection and intonation on different parts of the word and their reading doesn't make sense.

Lisa, who teaches in Florida where the Florida Comprehension Assessment Test (FCAT) wields power over all teaching decisions, knows that her students' scores on fluency assessments are considered more important than her professional knowledge:

Supposedly the numbers tell whether or not they are going to pass FCAT. The students who don't meet benchmarks are tutored with intensive work designed specifically as test prep. I have no input at all into what skills my students are tutored in, on what skills they may need to work on, what their interests are that might help them to build comprehension. I never see the tutoring plans, and no one asks for my input.

Lisa is not alone. In our positions as teacher educators and researchers we have interacted with hundreds of teachers, both preservice and inservice, who are facing the same challenges. Teachers frequently tell us they are leaving teaching—not because they don't like it but because testing and data-keeping have ruined their lives. Not only do teachers feel that the way they are forced to assess reading is harmful to their students, they see little value in the data they are required to report. Many teachers believe that the current overemphasis on fluency as a way to measure comprehension is counterproductive:

It changes their whole way of thinking when it comes to reading, especially reading out loud. They see no periods; they see no punctuation whatsoever. There's no intonation. They just fly right through it because they think they are just being timed. It's all about how fast you can read and they know that. Until we focus on building comprehension, our students don't have a chance at becoming real readers.

This book is our attempt to help teachers like Lisa who face daily struggles as they try to understand current mandates placed on them and their students. We, like Lisa, question whether there is sufficient scientific evidence to support the prominence of fluency in today's classrooms. What do we know about the role of fluency in the reading process? Has, as Allington (2002) warned, ideology trumped evidence? This book offers a much needed critical examination into what fluency is, how and why it has become a priority in national literacy policy, and whether there is sufficient evidence to support its current role in literacy education.

What Is Fluency and How Important Is It?

The title of Richard Allington's recent chapter, "Fluency: Still Waiting After All These Years" (2006), captures a reality in the field of reading research and instruction. Despite the focus on fluency in schools across the country, there continues to be no consensus regarding a definition of fluency or its role in overall reading proficiency. Fluency is a common word; and, like many common words, it's apt to have multiple meanings influenced by the specific contexts in which it is used. Despite formal endorsement of fluency as a pillar of reading in the Reading First section of No Child Left Behind (NCLB), there is still enormous variation in how it is described. Its meaning varies depending on who uses the word, their underlying assumptions about the nature of reading, their purpose for describing it, their methodologies for measuring it, and their intended audience.

In this chapter, we share various conceptualizations of fluency that align with multiple perspectives of the reading process. With the recent attention given to fluency instruction, educators are confronted with theoretical claims and research findings grounded in vastly different views of the reading process, ranging from transmission views to a transactional view. In an effort to bring some clarity to the fluency arena, we have developed a continuum that will help teachers to understand distinctions among differing perspectives, as well as the issues and controversies surrounding the focus on fluency in today's educational climate.

As reflected in Figure 2–1, we categorized various views of fluency under three major theories of the reading process: transmission, interactive, and transactional. Subsumed within a transmission theory are three distinct perspectives of reading and fluency: recoding, automaticity,

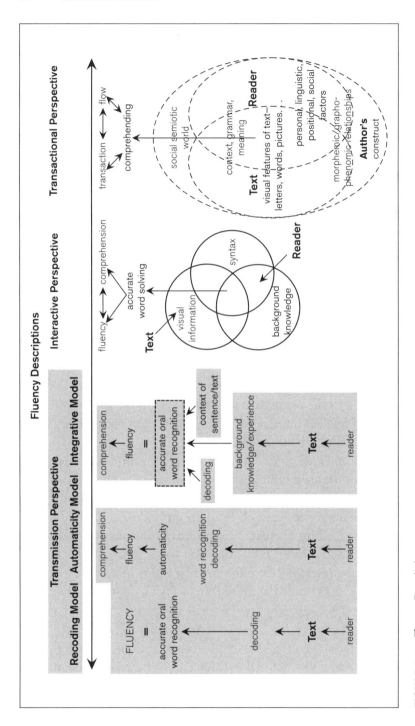

FIGURE 2–1. *Fluency Descriptions*

and integrative. Although the labels we have chosen for the various theories and perspectives are generally consistent with how they are used throughout the reading literature, there are some points of departure from particular fluency theorists (Fuchs et al. 2001), specifically in our use of the terms integrative and interactive. In what follows, we will therefore describe and differentiate among each perspective based upon our own understanding of reading theory and fluency research:

1. Recoding perspective: Reading equals the accurate translation of graphemic input into a phonological representation in order to access a word in a reader's oral vocabulary. Fluency is the speed and accuracy with which this written-oral recoding is achieved.
2. Automaticity perspective: Reading requires the effortless decoding of words that reserves a reader's attentional capacity for comprehension. Fluency reflects the level of automaticity with which readers can quickly and accurately decode the text.
3. Integrative perspective: Reading is the identification of words achieved through the use of background knowledge and context, as well as decoding. Fluency is the speed and accuracy of word identification that leads to comprehension.
4. Interactive perspective: Reading is the use of multiple linguistic and cognitive cues that result in accurate word identification and meaning construction. Fluency is facilitated by and reflective of comprehension.
5. Transactive perspective: Reading involves the construction of meaning resulting from the dynamic transaction among author, text, and reader within particular social contexts. Fluency is reconceptualized as flow, reflecting the variable rate with which a reader progresses through a text in the process of comprehending.

Recoding Perspective

Much of the confusion over what fluency is centers around the issue of fluency's relationship to meaning. Even the positioning of the word *meaning* is problematic. Meaning for recoding theorists is achieved by decoding printed words to oral language (Carnine, Silbert, and Kameenui 1997; Good and Kaminski 2002). Once children say the word, meaning is accessed from their oral vocabulary. For instance, Direct Instruction (Engelmann and Hanner 1995) lessons resemble the following:

TEACHER: Get ready to read all the words on this page without making a mistake. First word. (Snaps fingers)

STUDENTS: drove

TEACHER: Next word. (Snaps fingers)

STUDENTS: lark

TEACHER: Next word. (Snaps fingers)

STUDENTS: track

TEACHER: Try again. (Snaps fingers)

STUDENTS: track

TEACHER: Try again. (Snaps fingers)

STUDENTS: trick

TEACHER: Next word. (Snaps fingers)

The children decode and pronounce a word in unison at the teacher's prompting and move on to the next word; there is no discussion of word meaning because in this program the authors assume that once the word is pronounced the word is known.

The goal of instruction, then, is to enable early readers to identify sounds that match letter combinations quickly. This can be learned through decoding of both real and pseudo words. In this model, the goal is accurate decoding. For teachers this would mean that once our students can decode a text accurately and quickly (fluently), we would assume that they comprehended it as long as the words in the text are part of the reader's vocabulary. This perspective is reflected in the

Dynamic Indicators of Basic Early Literacy Skills (DIBELS) (Good and Kaminski 2002), a reading assessment commonly used across the United States. The appropriateness of DIBELS for assessing reading is the subject of Chapter 9.

Automaticity Perspective

From the automaticity perspective, rapid decoding skills lead to automatic word recognition, which in turn allows the reader to comprehend the text. The measurement of reading fluency is handled as if it is synonymous with automatic word recognition (automaticity), a prerequisite for comprehension. From this perspective decoding has an effect on comprehension but comprehension does not have an effect on decoding (LaBerge and Samuels 1974). LaBerge and Samuels contend that comprehension demands attention. It therefore can only be achieved when decoding becomes automatic and enables the skilled reader to reassign attention from the lower-level word identification processes to the resource-demanding comprehension task. To clarify, for LaBerge and Samuels, after readers become fluent (can automatically decode the text), the focus of reading can shift to comprehension. Even though this model predates contemporary theories of the reading process, it still undergirds many beliefs about fluency.

Integrative Perspective

The integrative perspective also considers fluency in terms of rate and accuracy, but accomplished through an integration of lower-level decoding skills with context and background knowledge. Fuchs et al. differentiate this perspective from automaticity in that the reader's mind is not waiting for decoding to take place before word meaning can be contextualized by the reader. Fuchs et al. further delineate between automaticity and integrative processes in that "rapid word recognition short-circuits the conscious-attention mechanism" (2001, 242) that LaBerge and Samuels claim is necessary to decode words in the automaticity model.

Researchers who fall under the three perspectives above ascribe to the use of rate and accuracy scores to measure fluency. Their research links measures of rate and accuracy with scores on standardized reading tests (Fuchs et al. 2001; Good and Kaminski 2002; Shin et al. 1992). Depending on the study, the standardized scores include subtests which may measure a range of decoding, spelling, vocabulary, and comprehension skills. The standardized comprehension tests usually have short passages with multiple-choice questions. In addition, these tests are timed. We contend that the ability to perform on timed assessments may be the common denominator underlying the relationship that some researchers have found between standardized comprehension tests and measures of fluency.

This ability to perform under timed conditions may also be an unacknowledged factor in one of the most prominent norming studies to date (Tindal and Hasbrouk 1992), in which the researchers normed words correct per minute (WCPM). Curriculum Based Measurement (CBM) studies that are grounded in Stan Deno's work also use WCPM as the metric to measure the number of words students can accurately read orally within a controlled period of time. Proponents of CBM have been in search of an assessment framework that is not only reliable and valid, but also one that is manageable within classroom environments (Fuchs and Fuchs 1999). And they are not alone. Recommended benchmarks of WCPM seem to be arbitrary: assessing a reader as fluent varies from one researcher to another. For example, a fluent score for end of second grade ranges from 60–90 WCPM words if following Blachowicz et al. (2006); 90 WCPM if following Barone, Hardman, and Taylor (2006); equal to or above 90 WCPM if using Good and Kaminski's benchmarks (2002); or 79–99 WCPM if one decides to use Hasbrouck and Tindal's (2006) norms as a guide. At times, recommended benchmarks vary even within a single publication. Shanahan (2006) recommends 60–80 WCPM at one point in his chapter, "Fluency in the context of literacy instruction," and 90 WCPM elsewhere in the same chapter! To complicate these conflicting WCPM norms, the importance of accuracy is stressed (Samuel 1992), but there is no consensus on what accuracy means. For example, Rasinski (1990) counts substitutions, insertions, mispronunciations, and omissions as errors. Shinn et al. (1992) allow repetition and insertions, but count omissions, substitutions, and mispronunciations as errors. Further, there is no agreement on how to score hesitations: Rasinski advocates giving a word prompt after a five-second hesitation; Downhower (1987) does not mention a time lapse before supplying the word; but others (Hasbrouck and Tindal 1992; Shinn et al. 1992) recommend a three-second lapse before providing a word prompt. Which is it?

Interactive Perspective

Fuchs et al. consider interactive and integrative perspectives equally. However, we differentiate between the two. Our points of departure lie in the reader's level of engagement with the text and the way fluency is assessed. We posit that a truly interactive perspective takes into account the complexity of the reading process and moves away from seeking word-level assessments of reading. As we characterize this perspective, assessing fluency extends beyond the word-level rate and accuracy focus and conceptualizes fluency as "reading in phrases, with appropriate intonation and prosody" (Allington 2006).

This view of fluency is reflected in the research conducted by Pinnell and colleagues (1995) that has come to be known as the 1992 NAEP study and produced the oral reading fluency scale in Figure 2–2.

This study found evidence of a relationship between fluency and comprehension. Unlike other studies for which students produced cold readings,

> Students were asked to read the passage aloud only after they had read the passage twice silently—once previously as a part of the main written assessment and once before answering the IRPR [Integrated Reading Performance Record] comprehension questions. The study was designed in this manner to facilitate students' abilities to read the passage aloud as fluently as possible. (Pinnell et al. 1995, 20)

By this third reading students were most likely able to generate an oral reading to match their earlier understanding. Even so, according to the IRPR findings, the oral renditions of the most fluent readers were not the most accurate. Some of these students changed words and syntax but kept the meaning intact. Accuracy was not found to be the most important variable. Deviations from the text (omissions, substitutions, changes that did not affect meaning) were analyzed qualitatively. Rather than restricting their view of fluency to accuracy, researchers were more concerned with how the deviations from the text affected meaning and whether or not they were self-corrected. Their findings

---

NAEP's Integrated Reading Performance Record Oral Reading Fluency Scale

Level 4   Reads primarily in larger, meaningful phrase groups. Although some regressions, repetitions, and deviations from text may be present, these do not appear to detract from the overall structure of the story. Preservation of the author's syntax is consistent. Some or most of the story is read with expressive interpretation.

Level 3   Reads primarily in three- or four-word phrase groups. Some smaller groupings may be present. However, the majority of phrasing seems appropriate and preserves the syntax of the author. Little or no expressive interpretation is present.

Level 2   Reads primarily in two-word phrases with some three- or four-word groupings. Some word-by-word reading may be present. Word groupings may seem awkward and unrelated to larger context of sentence or passage.

Level 1   Reads primarily word-by-word. Occasional two-word or three-word phrases may occur? But these are infrequent and/or they do not preserve meaningful syntax.

NAEP Report 1995

FIGURE 2–2. *NAEP's Integrated Reading Performance Record Oral Reading Fluency Scale*

showed that these deviations were important for meaning construction; and as a result, the research questioned the place of accuracy as one of the most salient variables in fluency.

Even though the 1992 NAEP study was based on a third exposure to a text, findings of the relationship between fluency and comprehension continue to be used by many researchers (Johnston 2006; Rasinski 2000; Ruetzel 2006) as justification for using rate and accuracy during the *first* reading of a text to assess overall reading proficiency.

Transactive Perspective

Goodman (1996), Rosenblatt (1994), Smith (1994), and Flurkey (1998) ascribe to a transactional perspective of reading that perceives meaning as constructed through a dynamic process. In this view, meaning cannot in any literal sense be in the signals or on the printed page but constructed anew through each transaction. Using social conventions and the context for the transaction, readers bring all their resources, purposes, and intentions to the text to construct a unique interpretation of it. With this dynamic vision of literacy in mind, consider Smith's description of a fluent reader:

> Experienced readers (when they are reading fluently) can easily identify individual words if they have to. They use nonvisual information in order to comprehend and are less dependent on the identification of individual words in the text or on the surrounding words. They "take control" of the text through the four characteristics of meaningful reading—their reading is purposeful, selective, anticipatory, and based on comprehension...Fluent reading is based upon a flexible specification of intentions and expectations, which change and develop as a consequence of the reader's progression through a text. Thus fluent reading demands knowledge of the conventions of the text, from vocabulary and grammar to the narrative devise employed. How much conventional knowledge is required depends of the purposes of the reading and the demands of the situation. (Smith 1994, 178)

Even the most fluent (experienced) readers will encounter difficulties reading some texts for which they may lack relevant knowledge, interests, or purposes. As Flurkey explains, "Different readers have different life experiences to bring to the text, and they may bring different linguistic resources to a literacy event. In short, no two individuals will read the same text at the same speed nor should they be expected to" (1998, 5).

Miscue analysis has been used to show a reader's efforts at negotiating the meaning of a text. It documents the unexpected responses (the ones that veer from the text) a reader makes during an oral reading of an authentic text. Analyses of these unexpected responses (miscues) provide a myriad of data about a reader and also give us insight into the nature of the reading process itself. Each of a reader's miscues tells us something. For example, some miscues that are self-corrected show that the reader is constructing meaning. Regressions or multiple attempts for a text segment may reflect that a reader is trying to create a meaningful structure. Meaningful omissions can be a reflection of a reader's efficiency of reading, while meaningful insertions may reflect the reader's more interesting elaboration of the author's text. As a whole, these miscues show a pattern, which allows inferences to be made about a reader and how they go about constructing meaning while reading. Goodman calls this "comprehending."

Flurkey takes miscue analysis a step further in augmenting it with an analysis of variations in the rate of reading throughout the reading of a text. Based on his research, he proposes to replace the term *fluency* (with its implicit reference to speed, accuracy, and expression) with the word *flow* to conceptualize the dynamic nature of reading within a "fluency as transaction" view. According to Flurkey, experienced readers produce few miscues that result in meaning change with familiar text; whereas, when even the most experienced reader confronts unfamiliar text or when a beginning reader approaches a text, regressions are more frequent. In addition, readers read more slowly "when their predictions are not confirmed by the visual cues they expect to see. As readers negotiate a particular text, it is common to hear them speed up and slow down as they respond to the text that they perceive" (1998, 6). Flurkey uses the definition "to follow a course" to describe this flow of "speed up and slow down." Combining miscue markings from transcripts with "observations of a reader's speed," he was able to "get a sense of a reader's dynamic response to text" or flow.

Conclusion

Clearly, there is no consensus regarding fluency's role in the reading process. Given that it is steeped in such theoretical debate, we must question how this concept has captured the uncontested support of the federal government. In our next chapter we will examine the fluency section of the National Reading Panel in an attempt to better understand how fluency has become mandated by NCLB and has become such a driving force in our schools.

Following the Fluency Trail
From the National Reading Panel to Reading First

In 1997 the federal government commissioned a group of researchers to conduct a meta-analysis of reading research. The commission's report, published in 2000 and called the National Reading Panel (NRP) Report, has changed the face of reading instruction throughout the United States. It has since been surrounded by controversy; reading researchers have debated its strengths and weaknesses for several years. In spite of this, the report has been endorsed as the voice of authority by federal reading policy makers and is the foundation for federal funding.

Adding to the complex problem that stems from the lack of agreement regarding the contents of the actual report are the publications that claim to be based on the NRP. These range from pamphlets distributed on the same website as the report itself to full volume interpretations of the findings in the NRP. These publications are widely disseminated to parents, teachers, and colleges of education.

Numerous reading research professionals have addressed the problems in the methods used by the NRP as well as their findings. It is beyond the scope of this chapter to address those critiques. Rather, at this point in our country's history of educational policy and practice, we feel it is most important to address the claims that support the commonly held assumption that the NRP's analysis of reading research identified fluency as a crucial factor in the reading process. This assumption is reinforced by the materials mentioned above that claim to be based on the findings of the NRP report.

The NRP Did Not Establish the Role of
Fluency in Successful Reading

The NRP is divided into six subgroup reports, each with its own set of authors. The fluency subgroup report was authored by S. J. Samuels, Timothy Shanahan, and Sally Shaywitz. The twenty-eight page report includes a five-page executive summary and is followed by fourteen pages of references. The stated objectives of the report are as follows:

> First, an overall introduction addresses the importance of the development of fluency in reading and provides background for two subsections. From that point, the report is organized in two major sections, with individual methods, results and discussion, implications for reading instruction and directions for future research. Finally, the Panel offers overall conclusions on extant research addressing reading fluency. (NICHD 2000, 3–5)

Before discussing the two instructional approaches the NRP subgroup analyzed, the report provides an historic overview of the varying theoretical understandings and definitions of fluency. It then provides an analysis of instructional strategies which may aid in the development of fluent reading. Although the NRP is often cited as having reviewed 100,000 studies, only 77 were selected to determine the effectiveness of teaching repeated oral reading. Given that there weren't enough studies of independent reading that fit their criteria, these findings are limited at best.

In the introduction, the subgroup's report states: "Fluent readers can read text with speed, accuracy, and proper expression" (NICHD 2000, 3–1). The report traces the changing definitions and theoretical perceptions of fluency but by and large supports an automaticity model. The importance of fluency in the reading process was addressed in this section. Two research studies are cited: *The National Assessment of Educational Progress* (NAEP) study published in 1995 (Pinnell et al.) and The National Research Council's *Preventing Reading Difficulties in Young Children* (Snow, Burns, and Griffin 1998).

Two critical points need to be made about these two studies that are not explicit in the report or the conclusions of the report. First, the NAEP study was conducted on fourth grade students. Second, the Snow study was "charged with conducting a study of the effectiveness of interventions for young children who are at risk of having problems learning to read" (Snow, Burns, and Griffin 1998, 1). Research cannot be generalized across groups of learners—findings for fourth grade readers cannot be applied to emergent readers and what is recommended for first grade children who are at risk should not be generalized to normally progressing learners. These basic tenets of research ethics are violated by the subgroup report.

Furthermore, the NRP advocates for an automaticity model of fluency while the NAEP study does not. The NAEP study rated fluency on a scale of 1–4 which included prosody as a primary indicator of a fluent reader. According to the NRP, the difference between a fluent and disfluent reader lies in their automatic processing:

> Skilled readers usually have several options available for word recognition. They can recognize words automatically or . . . they can use controlled effortful strategies to decode the word. Unskilled readers, on the other hand, are limited to controlled effortful word recognition. (3–9)

On the other hand, according to the NAEP study, much more than automatic word retrieval must be taken into consideration when assessing the fluency of a reader (see Chapter 2, Figure 2–2). The two constructs of fluency are very different, and it is not possible to transfer the findings of one to the other as if all measures of fluency are equal.

The claims made regarding fluency in the NRP report are at best theoretical. At no point in this section do the authors of the report cite any research beyond the NAEP study to establish a link between comprehension and fluency. They do not claim that fluency is a pillar of reading. The report does not claim that their statements are supported by research. Their position is most clearly made in this statement: "It is generally acknowledged that fluency is a critical component of skilled reading" (NICHD 2000, 3–1).

Secondary Documents: Distortion of the NRP Findings

The myth that the NRP has proven fluency to be a pillar of successful reading has grown in magnitude since the publication of the report. This has developed through misrepresentation of the report that began almost immediately after the report was released. One of the most significant distortions of the NRP is *Put Reading First: The Building Blocks of Reading Instruction, Kindergarten Through Grade Three* (Armbruster and Osborn 2001, 2003), now in its second edition. A disclaimer appears in both editions of this publication warning that "the comments or considerations do not necessarily represent the positions or policies of [the National Institute for Literacy] NIFL, [the Office of Educational Research and Improvement] OERI, U.S. Department of Education." Nevertheless, a direct link is drawn to these organizations on the page facing the disclaimer:

> This document was published by the Partnership for Reading, a collaborative effort of the National Institute for Literacy, the National Institute of Child Health and Human Development, and the U.S. Department of Education to make evidence-based reading research available to educators, parents, policy-makers, and others with an interest in helping all people learn to read well. The findings and conclusions in this publication were drawn from the 2000 report of the National Reading Panel, Teaching Children to Read: An Evidence-Based Assessment of the Scientific Research Literature on Reading and Its Implications for Reading Instruction–Reports of the Subgroups. (Armbruster and Osborn 2001, 2003, i)

The confusion over the legitimacy of this document is apparent to any reader. In addition to these printed contradictory claims, the document is distributed on the NRP's webpage (www.nationalreadingpanel. org/Publications/researchread.htm). Furthermore, other than the reference to the NRP report above, not a single citation of the NRP report or any other research can be found in the fifty-eight-page document.

Armbruster and Osborn's distortion of the NRP findings have had a significant impact on reading instruction in classrooms across the United States. Since this information is presented as a voice of authority and claims to be based on the NRP findings, it is therefore used as a reference source and teachers are expected to align their instruction to match the recommendations. A comparison of the two documents yields numerous contradictions regarding fluency instruction and assessment. Most significant are the inconsistencies in the definition of fluency and the recommendations for assessing fluency.

The first line in the NRP report, "Fluent readers can read text with speed, accuracy, and proper expression" (NICHD 2000, 3–1), sends a very different instructional message than the first line in the fluency section of *Put Reading First*: "Fluency is the ability to read a text accurately and quickly" (Armbruster and Osborn 2001, 22). *Put Reading First* shapes a way of thinking about fluency that was unsubstantiated in the NRP report or not studied at all. It claims (1) "Repeated and monitored oral reading improves reading fluency and overall reading achievement" (24) and (2) "No research evidence is available currently to confirm that instructional time spent on silent, independent reading with minimal guidance and feedback improves reading fluency and overall reading achievement" (23). In addition, teachers and parents are told that students need to practice their fluency using books with words they already know or can decode quite easily. This is not an NRP recommendation.

In contrast to the NRP report where no rate or accuracy scores were discussed, the use of accuracy scores is promoted and qualified in the *Put Reading First* document: independent is 95 percent accuracy, instructional is 90 percent accuracy, and frustration is less than 90 percent. Benchmarks for words correct per minute (WCPM) norms, according to *Put Reading First*, are ninety to one hundred for the end of second grade. Again, no WCPM benchmarks appear in the NRP report. And finally, this document states that silent reading should not be used in place of direct reading instruction because "reading fluency develops the most when students are working directly with you" (Armbruster and Osborn 2001, 2003, 29). Again, this statement would be difficult to prove using NRP data.

Reading First Section of No Child Left Behind (NCLB)

Regrettably, the distorted claims made by *Put Reading First* have made their way into classroom practice. Students' reading ability is now measured by WCPM and accuracy scores. The NRP fluency subgroup's characterization of fluency as "an essential part of reading" concludes with a strong call for more research, acknowledging that much still needs to be learned about the impact of guided oral reading on word recognition, fluency (speed and accuracy), and comprehension:

> There is a need for more research on this topic, including longitudinal studies that examine the impact of these procedures on

different levels of students over longer periods. It would also be
worthwhile to determine the amount of such instruction that
would be needed with most students and the types of materials
that lead to the biggest gains when these procedures are used.
(NICHD 2000, 3–28)

In spite of this clear and straightforward claim that more research is
needed, the federal government proclaimed fluency as one of "the five
key areas that scientifically based reading research has identified as essential components of reading instruction" and requires:

1. Professional development, instructional programs, and materials
   used by a state education agency (SEA) or school district must focus on the five key areas that scientifically based reading research
   has identified as essential components of reading instruction—
   phonemic awareness, phonics, vocabulary, fluency, and reading
   comprehension.
2. That all teachers have the skills they need to teach scientifically
   based instructional programs and to effectively screen, identify and
   overcome reading barriers facing their students. States will have significant funds to support professional development statewide, not
   just to school districts receiving Reading First subgrants. (U.S. Department of Education 2006, 11)

Consequently, based on dubious assumptions and insignificant data,
teaching and assessing fluency have become federal reading policy.

The Role of the Reading First Grant Funding Office

Even though there weren't enough studies to justify the "scientifically
based" conclusions in the NRP report, the Reading First section of NCLB
legislation still identifies fluency as one of the key components of reading and reading instruction and requires that funding be attached to implementation of reading programs with a so-called scientific base.

As we follow the trail from the NRP to current practice, the final
blow to all those who might still question the authenticity of the claims
that fluency is a pillar of the reading process came through the Federal
Reading First Grant Funding Office. In what has now been revealed
through the investigations conducted by the Office of the Inspector

General (OIG) of the United States Department of Education, the Reading First grant funding process has been steeped in corruptions since its inception. The OIG Reports (ED-OIG/A03G0006; ED-OIG/I13-F0017) reveal a grant funding process that forced states to adopt programs that were selected by individuals who stood to benefit financially from the adoption process.

> Specifically, we found that: 1) the "Theory to Practice" sessions at the RLAs [Reading Leadership Academies] focused on a select number of reading programs; and 2) the RLA Handbook and Guidebook appeared to promote the Dynamic Indicators of Basic Early Literacy Skills (DIBELS) Assessment Test. With regard to RMC Research Corporation's (RMC) technical proposal for the NCRFTA [National Center for Reading First Technical Assistance] contract, we concluded that the Department did not adequately assess issues of bias and lack of objectivity when approving individuals to be technical assistance providers before and after the NCRFTA contract was awarded.

In other words, federally sponsored reading academies that were supposed to be opportunities for state education leaders to learn how to implement the new federal policies were instead propaganda sessions that supported two reading instruction programs, Open Court and SRA Reading Mastery, and one assessment program, DIBELS. School districts did not have a choice—they either adopted fluency as a pillar of reading or lost federal funding for their schools.

S. J. Samuels: Fluency Is Not Just Rate and Accuracy

Many reading researchers, teachers, and parents continually question the implementation of NCLB, including the strict policies surrounding Reading First. Part of the outcry resulted in the OIG reports cited above, but even this widespread corruption has failed to initiate a change in reading policy at the federal level. Some voices are completely ignored and have never been invited to the table to discuss reading policy and practice.

But one voice among the many who have given service to the NRP and those creating federal policy should be revisited. At the International Reading Association's Fifty-First Annual Convention in Chicago, Illinois, S. Jay Samuels (2006) participated in a panel discussion addressing critical issues in reading education. Considering that Samuels is one of the three authors of the fluency section of the NRP, his message during this presentation is of extreme importance. At that time, Samuels shared his concerns with the audience, noting that the wording of the definition of fluency in the NRP report should have been more focused on prosody. He stated, "Speed is not a good indicator of reading proficiency." In reference to the definition of fluency in the NRP report, he commented, "I screwed up on it. The real definition should be 'Can you read a text and understand it at the same time?'"

Unfortunately, those in the position to act on Samuels' advice either were not in the audience or have not chosen to act.

How Can Young Readers Inform Us About Fluency?

In our roles as classroom teachers, reading specialists, and university professors over the years, we have had numerous opportunities to observe children engaged in school reading activities. Since the assessment of student learning has been central to our teaching and curricular decisions, we have devoted much of our professional lives to studying and using a wide range of literacy assessments including miscue analysis, running record, and curriculum-based assessments. Our considerable experience and knowledge have taught us the limited value of standardized test scores in helping us understand our students as readers and writers.

In recent years, we have witnessed the rise to prominence of fluency instruction and assessment in schools under the Reading First guidelines of No Child Left Behind (NCLB). In many schools, one-minute fluency assessments have replaced other analyses of student reading (close observation, miscue analysis, running record, work sampling, and parent feedback) that we consider more valuable for understanding and responding to students' unique reading needs. Yet we have found a lack of independent research providing scientific evidence (beyond standardized test scores) for this shift toward fluency assessment. As supervisors of student interns in area schools, we have also observed classrooms where, due to the fluency instruction and assessment craze, children are pressured to read faster and faster. Along with our student interns, we became concerned about the potential consequences of fluency-boosting practices our interns were expected to implement in their school placements. We realized that it was critical, not just for theoretical reasons but for current and future students and teachers, to more firmly examine the role of fluency in the reading process and in reading development.

But how could this be accomplished in a climate where mandates attached to funding have silenced or ignored many voices, including our own, and where debate and inquiry have been curtailed? As teachers and scholars, we felt that our best option was to conduct research. We strongly believed that claims made by politicians, consultants, textbook companies, administrators, and the director of National Institute of Child Health and Human Development (NICHD) about the importance of fluency needed to be subjected to scientific examination. Therefore we set up our study to conduct that examination and provide the field with further data that would help to assess the validity of these claims. We hoped to use our findings to inform our own teaching and to inform others who are impacted by current federal policies on fluency. And so we embarked on our journey.

Fortunately, we had already generated a wealth of data that provided us with the opportunity to conduct our inquiry. As members of a team of literacy researchers at Towson University, we had developed a study to respond to the proliferation of scripted, skill-based reading programs that were being mandated across our state under new system policies. We designed a research project to examine the impact of four contrasting reading programs, two of which represented the commercial programs that were being mandated and two of which were noncommercial literature-based programs. More specifically, these four reading programs were McGraw-Hill's SRA Reading Mastery [Direct Instruction] (Engelmann et al. 1995)]; McGraw-Hill's Open Court (2000); a county-developed literature-based reading program; and a guided reading program loosely based upon Fountas and Pinnell's model (1996). The primary levels of both McGraw-Hill programs focused predominantly on systematic phonics and skills for the teaching of reading. Both the literature-based and guided reading programs approach reading instruction as a holistic, meaning-based process. We hoped that our research would provide us with urgently needed information regarding the impact of contrasting reading programs on students' development of the reading process, including their comprehension, strategies, and the use of phonics both in and out of context. (See Altwerger et al. 2004, Altwerger 2005, and Wiltz and Wilson 2005 for further information on our findings.)

The theoretical tenet guiding our research design was that oral and written language are complex and socially constructed systems that cannot be fully understood without consideration of their intricate relationships to situated contexts. This intricacy and complexity is not taken into account in reading research based solely in quantitative experimental design. Therefore we created a methodology that would enable us to achieve an in-depth and multifaceted investigation of how students in various instructional programs develop as readers. Accordingly, we examined the impact of these four different reading programs using both quantitative and qualitative methods for data collection and analysis.

Approximately thirty children from each of the four program sites participated in the study. We selected a stratified random sample from all potential participants that teachers and/or schools identified as high, middle, or low readers. This enabled us to investigate relationships and distinctions among groups of students considered to be at varied levels of reading competence within and across program sites. This also helped us to examine the validity of grouping and labeling readers using running record accuracy scores and Open Court and Direct Instruction assessments. All of the participants were carefully screened to ensure that they had been taught using their respective reading program for a minimum of two years, were proficient English speakers, and received no special education services. Also, the children participating in the study were matched across school sites for percentages of free and reduced lunch (87 to 100 percent).

For the qualitative component of our study, we included classroom observations, literacy artifacts, and interviews with students and teachers. Our intent was to describe in detail the ecology of the classrooms so that we would be able to draw comparisons across programs in ways that gave us some understanding of how students construct knowledge about texts and the process of reading.

Our quantitative data included reading samples collected from each participant. Given that we hoped to generate representative samples of children's oral reading and comprehension of challenging, but not frustrating texts, we carefully selected books that spanned eight reading levels (kindergarten through fourth grade) based upon the gradient developed by Fountas and Pinnell's (1996, 2001) lists of leveled books. Each book had an identifiable story structure. We included three books at each level to be sure we had at least one selection that would be unfamiliar to each reader. Students were offered the selection of books that were deemed to be on or close to their instructional levels (based upon teacher recommendation and researcher judgment formed in the initial stages of the research sessions). Following miscue analysis protocol (Goodman, Watson, and Burke 1987), each student was then asked to read the target book aloud (without researcher assistance) and provide an unaided and aided oral retelling of the story. Each reading and retelling event was audiotaped to ensure accuracy and allow for reliable and precise coding of data. For each of these oral readings, we conducted a complete miscue analysis.

As discussed in Chapter 2, a miscue is defined as a reader's deviation from a written text while reading aloud. Miscue analysis generates an assessment of these deviations in order to document how readers integrate the cueing systems: graphophonic, the set of relationships between oral and written language; syntactic, the grammatical interrelationships of words and sentences; and semantic, the meanings of words and text. For our study, the researchers listened closely to students' oral readings during the research sessions, noting miscues and other pertinent behaviors on their printed copies of the stories (worksheets). We later returned to the audiotaped version of the readings to more completely mark the worksheets. For example, in Figure 4–1 the reader uses repetition (repeats what has already been read) as she reads. These parts are underlined and marked with ⓡ and are not considered miscues. In line 07 04 the reader read *they* for *I* and then self-corrected. The worksheet was marked with *I* underlined and *they* written above it and then marked as a self-correction ⓒ (see Figure 4–1).

From these marks, a coding sheet was completed which analyzed the miscue in order to note the reader's use of cueing systems and strategies. Another researcher independently listened to the tape and coded the miscues. Interrater reliability was established for the coding of miscues at .90. Miscue data was analyzed for syntactic acceptability, semantic acceptability, meaning change, correction, meaning construction, grammatical relationship, sound similarity, and graphic similarity. For each miscue, researchers rated the extent to which the miscues reflected these variables. For example, a substitution miscue could have HIGH, SOME, or NO graphic or sound similarity to the text word; that miscue could also be fully semantically or syntactically acceptable (Y), partially acceptable (P), or not acceptable at all (N). From the codings of each miscue for each reader, percentages were calculated (see Figure 4–2).

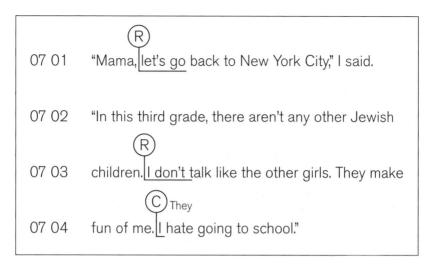

FIGURE 4–1. *Example of Miscue*

For the retelling analysis, a retelling scoring sheet was created for each story. Students' retellings were scored independently by two researchers, through first an unaided retelling and then an aided retelling. Retelling scores were determined based on the identification of setting, characters, theme, and plot episodes; on retelling cohesion; and on the inferences/connections that were made. Again, raw scores were used to calculate a percentage for each retelling.

Advocates of phonics-based programs claim that these programs are better at teaching phonics skills to decode words in isolation and to decode words in extended text. We decided to test this claim. Therefore, in addition to the miscue analysis that assesses the use of graphophonic cues while reading authentic texts, we also administered the Woodcock Johnson Psycho-Educational Battery-R (WJPE-R) Word Attack subtest (Woodcock and Bonner Johnson 1990). This provided a standardized assessment of the children's ability to apply phonics knowledge in isolation.

The data from the miscue analysis and the phonics test were then analyzed using multivariate statistics. Findings were examined in relation to the qualitative data collected at each program site (classroom observations, literacy artifacts, and student and teacher interviews), thereby providing us with a multidimensional and comprehensive picture of the children as readers.

Reader	Text	Syntactic acceptability			Semantic acceptability			Meaning change			Correction			Meaning Construction			Strength	Partial strength	Overcorrection	Weakness	Grammatical relationship	Sound similarity			Graphic similarity		
		Y	P	N	Y	P	N	Y	P	N	Y	P	N	No loss	Partial loss	Loss						H	S	N	H	S	N
	they	✓					✓	✓			✓			✓			✓							✓			✓
Column total																											
Pattern total																											
Percentage																											

FIGURE 4–2. Miscue Analysis Coding Form

Our observations, literacy artifacts, and interviews confirmed that the teachers had implemented the respective programs. The Direct Instruction and Open Court programs resembled each other in that both devoted time each day to systematic, explicit phonics instruction, used books with stories or texts that progress from one level to the next, and provided lessons that established an instructional ritual: "Children sit through hours and hours of these repetitive reading lessons—new words, different stories, the same chant" (Jordan 2005). The Direct Instruction program, written by the publisher's in-house authors, controls the vocabulary that is introduced. Each new lesson builds on the one before it by introducing new words and utilizing previously taught phonic elements. Children answer questions in unison or individually. The questions can most often be answered with one word. For example, "What is the name of the store?" And there is always a snap and a recitation. Speed and accuracy are drilled. The Open Court program differs from the Direct Instruction program in that some time is also allocated to teach children to ask questions, to predict and confirm, to use background knowledge, and to make inferences as they read. Nevertheless, there is still only one correct answer, and often that requires just a single word response.

Like the two commercial phonics-based programs, the programs using literature for instruction (guided reading program and literature-based program) resembled each other in important ways. First, the reading lessons focused on constructing meaning from text. Children were taught and encouraged to use multiple language cues, including graphophonics, in order to comprehend while reading. Read-alouds, guided reading lessons (Fountas and Pinnell), the reading of authentic literature, and literature discussions were part of the daily plan. In addition, both programs had a writing component. These programs differed in that the guided reading program relied heavily upon leveled books (Fountas and Pinnell) for most of the instruction, whereas the literature-based program made children's self-selection of reading material central to the program. At times, the teacher did select multiple copies of authentic texts for guided reading lessons. Other times, groups' books were selected by the children themselves. While the children in the guided reading program were given topics and structures for their writing, the teachers in the literature-based program used a process approach for the teaching of writing which permitted students to choose their own topics and forms for their writing.

The most significant difference between these two literature-based programs was the amount of time children actually spent reading and writing. In this particular version of a guided reading program, children read connected text an average of only four minutes and fifteen seconds each day (over the course of our observation period). This included time spent reading during their guided reading lessons with the teacher and independent reading tasks. They wrote connected text for even less time. The rest of the language arts block consisted mostly of teacher-directed lessons dealing with how to use language cues to read. In contrast, teachers in the literature-based program devoted at least thirty minutes a day to children's silent independent reading and gave at least another thirty minutes to children for writing. In this program teachers took cues from their students and would allow more time for silent reading and for writing when children seemed actively engaged.

Research Extended to Investigate Fluency

With the above study complete (see Chapter 7 for a discussion of the results), members of the original research team divided into subgroups to focus on different areas of inquiry raised by our first set of findings. As criticisms of the National Reading Panel report's conclusions began to build, including those related to phonics, fluency, and comprehension, (Allington 2002; Coles 2003; Garan 2001; Graves 2001; Krashen 2001; Yatvin 2002), and as our concerns over changes to observed reading practices increased, we decided to make fluency the focus of our next inquiry. We turned to our initial data set, which we recognized as containing the resources we needed (audiotaped readings and retellings) to begin our investigation into the role fluency plays in the reading process.

After a thorough review of the research on fluency, both historical and current (see Chapter 2), we planned a study that would investigate fluency as it is widely being operationalized in policy and practice: as *oral reading rate and accuracy.* We posed the following questions:

1. What is the relationship between reading rate and accuracy and use of graphophonics in and out of context?
2. What is the relationship between reading rate and accuracy and meaning construction during reading?

3. What is the relationship between reading rate and accuracy and comprehension of text?
4. What is the relationship of reading rate and accuracy to meaning and comprehension for readers of high and low proficiency?
5. Do currently mandated commercial phonics-based programs develop reading rate and accuracy better than literature-based programs?

To address these questions, we analyzed all of the audiotaped oral readings accessible to us from the original study (108 oral readings) using four fluency assessment variables we developed specifically for this study. These included words per minute (WPM), or the number of words read during the first minute of reading; words correct per minute (WCPM), or the number of words read correctly during the first minute of reading (currently the most common measure of fluency); WPMmis, or the words read per minute for the text portion in which miscues had been analyzed (enabling us to examine rate and accuracy in relation to other miscue variables); and WPMtext, or the words read per minute for the entire story (allowing us to note any discrepancies between fluency results for the miscue section and the first minute).

Interrater reliability was established by having two researchers independently time each reading, with any differences resolved by a third and joint timing. For the data analysis, Pearson Correlation coefficients were generated to examine the relationships among measures of reading rate and accuracy, miscue analysis variables, and the phonics scores. MANOVA was used to examine differences among various groups of readers, such as high and low retellers, on measures of rate, accuracy, strategy use, and comprehension.

Fluency Assessment: DIBELS

Currently, one of the most widely used forms of early literacy assessment is the Dynamic Indicators of Basic Early Literacy Skills, or DIBELS (Good and Kaminski 2002). DIBELS claims to be a complete literacy assessment tool that can be used to make instructional recommendations. In our work with teachers in schools across the nation, we have found that students are being "DIBELED" at an escalating rate. In fact, it seems that the DIBELS Oral Reading Fluency (DORF) test has become one of the most influential programs for grouping and planning instruction for students. Therefore, we extended our research to include a case-study model of one additional classroom that reflected current practice related to fluency and which used the DIBELS assessment. For this part of our research we asked the following questions:

1. What is the relationship between DORF's measures of rate and accuracy to the same student's rate and accuracy of reading trade books?
2. What is the relationship between DORF and comprehension of literature texts?

As we explained earlier, several small inquiry groups formed from the larger group of researchers in order to investigate specific aspects of the reading process. One of these groups investigating text features (Martens, Arya, Wilson, and Jin 2005) collected new data that replicated our earlier study, audiotaping a group of readers at the end of their second-grade year and conducting a miscue analysis complete with retelling protocol. Since their research focus was on the impact of text features on comprehension, they increased the number of texts read by each participant in the study. Thus, their data set included miscue analyses of multiple readings and retellings for twenty-three readers.

Using this set of audiotaped readers, we replicated our fluency data collection techniques described above, generating rate and accuracy scores for thirteen additional readers for whom DIBELS Oral Reading Fluency (DORF) and Retelling Fluency (RTF) scores were made available. Our findings are reported in Chapter 9.

As we have described, our fluency study is uniquely positioned to provide us with needed information regarding the relationships among various aspects of the reading process, including reading rate, accuracy, comprehension, and the use of phonics both in and out of context. What then did second graders teach us about fluency when it is defined as rate and accuracy? Our findings provide powerful answers to the critical questions we should all be asking about fluency.

What Is the Relationship Between Fluency and Comprehension?

What is comprehension? Is it being able to talk about what you read? To answer multiple-choice or essay questions (or both) about a reading? Or is comprehension the general building of knowledge that develops our thinking—not just about details in reading, but details in life? Is comprehension static, a fixed product of reading? Or do you think of comprehension as comprehending—an ongoing process of understanding? What would it take for someone to prove to you that he has comprehended a text? It may seem odd for you to think about these questions, but it's very important to do so before reading further in this chapter.

Comprehension: An Active Process

Reading comprehension is the act of meaning-making while reading. While this seems simple enough, understanding how readers make meaning is not so simple. Reading teachers often refer to this meaning-making as active comprehension. Reading researchers have developed various models of comprehension to help teachers not only understand the comprehension process, but also to help identify effective models of comprehension instruction.

Transmission, interactive, and transactional are three of the most common views of comprehension. The transmission model of comprehension posits that meaning is found in the text and that there is only one correct reading of a text. The interactive model views reading comprehension as a process in which the reader takes meaning from the text and adds her own meaning to arrive at an understanding, or comprehension, of the text. In the transactional view of reading comprehension, meaning is in the author and meaning is in the reader; the text is an attempt to reflect meaning and has the potential to become meaningful in the hands of the reader. Alone, without the reader, the text only has intention and potential. This view of reading comprehension proposes that the text and the reader's experience and background combine in the process of reading, and meaning is constructed based on a transaction between the two. Thus, comprehension is a fluid process, a transaction.

Regardless of which definition of comprehension you prefer, we presume you would agree that reading comprehension is the result of reading behaviors that are not in and of themselves measurable. In other words, we cannot visibly see what is taking place in the brain of a reader while she is in the act of comprehending a text. Nevertheless, the resulting product of the act of thinking is sometimes believed to be measurable in terms of, among other things, question and answering practices, discussion, illustration and other forms of artistic expression, various forms of writing, and a host of other response-type "comprehension" measures or activities.

According to Goodman (1994, 31), "The distinction between comprehending as a process and comprehension as a product is important and useful . . . Since comprehending is a constructive process in which readers make sense of the text, it occurs while reading and even long afterwards as the reader reconsiders and reconstructs what has been comprehended; thus comprehension may be changed in the course of testing it." Therefore, it is safe to say that comprehending is the process of constructing meaning during reading, while comprehension is the resulting product of comprehending.

When understanding reading comprehension and its relationship to oral reading, researchers and teachers work from an intuitive sense that fluent oral reading is an indicator of successful reading. We assume that when students read faster and with greater accuracy, and perhaps more expressively, that comprehension follows. From this assumption a focus on fluency has developed and the role of reading fast and accurately has come to be a definitive indication of comprehension. As noted in Chapter 2, however, research has not established a correlational or causal link between comprehension and fluency outside of testing conditions.

In order to formally investigate this critically important link between the qualities of oral reading and comprehension, we must first make clear our qualitative understanding of both comprehending and comprehension.

Comprehending: Meaning Construction While Reading

Goodman's work brought detailed understanding of oral reading behaviors. Rather than understanding utterances that differ from what is written on the page as errors, for the first time teachers and researchers began to understand the value of qualifying these errors as miscues. Miscues are examined and analyzed to determine which cueing systems (such as graphophonic, semantic, syntactic) the reader utilized while processing and making sense of continuous text. All miscues are not equal according to miscus analysis; the type of miscue made during oral reading is examined and qualified. For a more complete description of miscue analysis, see Goodman, Watson, and Burke (2005). Simply speaking, graphophonic cues reveal the reader's use of the sound/letter relationship or the phonic system; syntactic cues reveal a reader's use of the grammatical structure of language—such things as noun/verb order, word endings, function words, and other structural features; and semantic cues reveals the reader's use of word and sentence meaning. Semantic cues receive the most attention in this chapter because they help us to examine the link between meaning-making or comprehending while reading and fluency.

Comprehension: Retelling

The retelling procedures of miscue analysis conceive of readers' oral retellings of texts they have read as "parallel stories" (Goodman, Watson, and Burke 2005, 51). As such, teachers and researchers quantify and qualify "Readers' responses to text [to] provide insights into the depth and breadth of their comprehension" (55). Teachers and researchers prepare retelling guides that include the elements of fiction (e.g., characterization, setting, plot, theme) for narrative text and specific and general information for expository text (e.g., facts, principles, concepts). The retelling is quantitatively and qualitatively assessed and scored in relation to the retelling guide.

Comprehension, though not static, is the result of comprehending. During the initial phase of the retelling protocol readers recall as much about the text as they can without specific prompting. This is different from many classroom procedures where readers interact in directed reader response—either through discussion, answering questions, or specific written responses. Since the act of comprehending continues even after the reading has been completed (Pressley 1998), it is important to point out that the retelling protocol used in this research includes both unaided and aided retelling. Aided retellings use open-ended questions to flesh out specific details that the reader may have left out of the unaided retelling. They provide the opportunity for readers who are not familiar with retelling protocols to elaborate their shared retelling, thus ensuring as accurate a measure of comprehension as possible.

Our Findings: Oral Reading and Comprehension

Meaning Construction Variables: Comprehending

The interpretation and evaluation of miscues allow us to address important questions regarding the reading behaviors of the students in this study. Examining meaning construction variables provides insight into the process of comprehending, and comparing those variables with measures of rate and accuracy gives us the ability to determine if there is a relationship between comprehending during reading and measures of rate and accuracy of reading.

In order to determine if there were significant correlations between comprehending and various measures of fluency, we conducted a statistical analysis of our data. We compared several meaning construction variables (semantic acceptability, meaning construction, and correction) to several fluency variables. Recall from Chapter 4 that we developed the following fluency variables:

Words per Minute (WPM)
Words Correct per Minute (WCPM)
Words per Minute in Miscue Section (WPMmis)
Words per Minute in the Story (WPMtext)

Our findings revealed no correlation between measures of fluency and semantic acceptability or correction for the students in our study. In other words, the miscues of readers who read faster and more accurately did not reflect greater semantic acceptability or correction strategies than less fluent readers.

For three of the four schools there was no correlation between the variables of meaning construction and fluency. However, there was a significant relationship found for the literature-based school that will be discussed in Chapter 7.

Comprehension Variable

In order to examine the relationship between fluency and retelling, correlations were run between those variables. No statistically significant correlation was found between WCPM and retelling. We also examined the data for significant differences among homogeneous subsets of readers based on fluency scores. We found no significant difference in retelling scores among these groups of students. Faster and more accurate readers do not have significantly higher retelling scores, and slower, less accurate readers do not have significantly lower retelling scores.

Moving away from the statistical analysis and examining individual readers can help us understand the lack of statistical difference between these variables. In our data set, many readers who were fast and accurate also comprehended well. But the reverse also holds true: many slow readers also comprehend well. Furthermore, a number of fast and accurate readers were unable to retell what they read and exhibited little or no comprehension of the text. In fact, when lining up the retelling scores next to the words correct per minute no pattern emerges at all. For example, the student in this study who reads with the highest comprehension scored 93 percent on her retelling, but only read at a rate of 40 WCPM. Two students who both scored 88 percent, among the highest retelling scores, reflect the kind of differences found across the data set: one of those readers read at a rate of 104 WCPM, while the other read at 40 WCPM.

It is not just the high-scoring retellers who show this kind of range of rate and accuracy. The variation can be best illustrated by examining the five lowest retelling scores: 14, 21, 23, 27, and 29. A total of ten students generated these scores; two students scored 23 percent and four scored 29 percent. In this group of ten students, the fluency scores range from 35 to 118 WCPM.

Conclusions

Much research confirms the importance of meaning construction during reading as well as the value of retelling in understanding a reader's comprehension. This research base is scientifically rigorous and has withstood the scrutiny of reading researchers from many theoretical perspectives. Studies that support measures of rate and accuracy as indicators of reading comprehension do not have the same strong peer-reviewed research foundation. As noted in Chapter 2, the link between comprehension and fluency is a theoretical link, not a research-evidenced link. Furthermore, much of the research that established oral reading norms (Hasbrouck and Tindal 1992, 2006) did not consider any measure of comprehension and yet claims to be important in making instructional decisions. Our research reveals that the most commonly used measures of fluency—rate and accuracy—do not help us determine who may or may not actively construct meaning during or after reading.

The findings of this research suggest that using current fluency norms for assessing students' reading proficiency in relationship to comprehension presents serious problems. Teachers in this study identified student reading levels and made instructional decisions on the basis of rate and accuracy, but not comprehension.

Some assessment measures, most notably DIBELS, correlate rate and accuracy with standardized test scores. As discussed in Chapter 2, there are problems with the research that supports this practice. These studies use only standardized testing as a measure of reading comprehension. This is problematic in that both rate and accuracy measures and standardized tests are timed performances. Thus, time—not thinking ability or reading proficiency—can be the determining factor in success or failure on the tests.

Furthermore, we know from many years of research that reading rate varies with the type and purpose of reading (Pressley 1998) as well as across a single text (Flurkey 1998; Goodman 1994). Placing rate and accuracy at the forefront of reading assessment and instructional practices will undoubtedly influence young readers to read more quickly (Allington 1983). But our research suggests that this will not necessarily lead to comprehension.

In light of this, it should not be surprising that the data shared in this study do not, in any way, support the notion that rate and accuracy indicates the quality of the reader's comprehending or comprehension. What we do know is that teachers place students in reading levels, grouping them for instruction, based on their presumed proficiency. Too often this is determined by how fluently they sound, which tells very little about how well they comprehend.

What Is the Relationship Between Fluency and Decoding?

As we discussed in Chapter 2, many fluency researchers and theorists consider the ability to identify words rapidly and accurately as critical to fluent reading. In turn, fluent reading is considered either prerequisite to or synonymous with comprehension (an assumption that we challenged in the last chapter). But despite some disagreement concerning the fluency-comprehension relationship, there is almost unanimous agreement that rapid and immediate decoding of printed words to sounds is foundational to both fluency and comprehension. Ehri (1998), for example, posits that fluency develops as a result of achieving increasingly higher stages of alphabetic knowledge until, at the Fully and Consolidated Alphabetic Stages, children have developed enough decoding skill to read words automatically without undue attention. That attention may therefore be devoted to comprehension. Although Ehri considers vocabulary development and other linguistic factors as contributing to the full achievement of fluency, she still considers the ability to decode print to sound using a highly developed understanding of the alphabetic principle as prerequisite. Pikulski and Chard (2005), while suggesting a "deep" understanding of fluency that incorporates comprehension in its definition, still regard phonic decoding as essential: "Fluency builds on a foundation of oral language skills, phonemic awareness, familiarity with letter forms, and efficient decoding skills" (517).

Once again we find ourselves strategically positioned to examine some givens in the fluency literature, this time in terms of the various relationships between phonics and fluency, and phonics and comprehension. The 108 students in our study provide us with the means to test many of the hypotheses and assumptions that have found their way into classroom instruction and assessment, including:

- Fluency is dependent upon skill in using phonics to decode words.
- The ability to decode print out of context transfers to the high use of graphophonic cues in the context of reading and consequently to greater fluency.
- The ability to comprehend text is dependent upon a high level of decoding skill in and out of context.
- Highly competent decoders are better able to read with comprehension.

As you will recall, we have several variables that provide us with the information we need for our inquiry. The miscue analysis generates variables that assess the extent to which a word substitution looks like and sounds like the text word. A miscue can have either high, some, or no graphic similarity to the text word, as well as high, some, or no sound similarity. For example, a substitution of the word *a* for *the* has some sound similarity but no graphic similarity to the text word. The substitution of *tough* for *though* has high graphic similarity, but no sound similarity to the text word. Graphic and sound similarity is analyzed separately in order to more precisely capture the cues readers use: Is a reader using letters to predict a word that looks like the text word, or using the sounds associated with the letters in the word to "sound it out"? In many oral reading assessments, these two variables are collapsed under the umbrella of phonic analysis.

In addition to the miscue analysis variables that tell us how readers are using graphic and sound (graphophonic) cues during the actual reading of text, we also have data on each reader's performance on the Woodcock Johnson Psycho-Educational Battery-R (WJPE-R) Word Attack subtest (Woodcock and Bonner Johnson 1990). This test requires that students use their knowledge of letter-sound relationships to sound out a list of pseudo words. Because the list contains no real words that students may already know, it is considered a test of pure phonic knowledge. The test administrator records a raw score of pseudo words "read" correctly. This is then converted to a standard score and a percentile rank that represents a comparison of that student's performance to the normed population of the same grade and month.

All of these variables are then subjected to statistical analyses along with measures of comprehending, comprehension, and fluency

(WCPM) to determine whether and how they are interrelated for different types of readers. Although we have already discussed our results concerning the relationships we found between meaning construction and fluency variables in Chapter 5, in this chapter we will examine the relationship of phonic and graphophonic knowledge to both fluency and meaning. If our results challenge commonly held beliefs regarding these relationships, we may need to rethink the current emphasis on phonics instruction and assessment. So let's examine each of the claims and assertions listed earlier, one at a time.

Fluency is dependent upon skill in using phonics to decode words.

The first analysis we conducted gave us a general look at whether there is any relationship between results on the Woodcock-Johnson subtest (which we will call phonics) and words correct per minute (WCPM), our measure of fluency. Results of the correlation between these variables indicate a mild but significant correlation (r=.43). This means that for the entire data set there is a positive relationship between fluency and phonics. This finding does not, however, provide us with specific information on why or how the variables are related. Mild correlations can reflect a general but not systematic relationship and may hold for some, but not all, of the data. We therefore decided to look more closely at our results to see whether students with high and low phonics scores also had consistently high and low fluency scores (as a significant correlation would suggest). Did the readers with high WCPM rates have consistently high phonics scores, or was there a great deal of variation? Did the students with higher phonics scores consistently have high WCPM rates, or was there a great deal of variation for this as well?

These are important questions to consider because if there is a high percentage of students who read fluently (with high rate and accuracy) but don't have high levels of phonic knowledge (as reflected on the phonics test), this would challenge the assumption that phonics is a prerequisite of fluency. If there are students with high phonic skill who still do not read quickly and accurately, then we would need to consider factors beyond decoding that facilitate fluency.

Looking first at our findings on the students with high WCPM rates (ninety and above), we find a mean phonics percentile rank of 77.93, meaning they performed better than three-quarters of the second graders in the normed group. That is quite high and consistent with the positive correlation we found earlier. When we take a closer look at the range of scores (and standard deviation from the mean), however, we see a wide range of phonic competencies for these students. The standard deviation was 29.1 (very high), with phonics percentiles ranging from the 17th to the 99th. In other words, there are some fast and accurate readers in our study who, for whatever reason, did not demonstrate phonic skill on the standardized phonics test consistent with the average second grader nationwide.

Turning to the slower, less accurate readers (below 70 WCPM), we find that they have a mean percentile rank of 50.86 on phonics, indicating that they performed smack in the middle in comparison to second graders in the normed group. This is significantly lower than the mean percentile rank in phonics for the more fluent readers. Once again, however, we see a large range of phonics scores for the less fluent readers, ranging from 2 to 99.8 (the highest phonics score in the study!). There are many other students (20 percent of them) with scores that lie above the 50th percentile on phonics, or better than half the second graders, and some (about 10 percent of them) with scores that were better than 75 percent of the normed second graders.

Although there was a significant difference between the average phonics scores of the least fluent readers and all the rest of the readers, we cannot assume that fluency is reliant upon highly skilled decoding ability. In other words, our study suggests that kids who are highly fluent readers are not necessarily great decoders and kids who are less fluent readers are not necessarily poor decoders.

To further explore the fluency-decoding relationship, we turned our analysis upside down and looked closely at the students with phonics scores in the highest and lowest 25th percentiles. For the students with the highest phonics scores (75th percentile and higher) we found a mild but significant correlation ($r=.43$) with their fluency scores. Despite this statistical significance, we noted a very large variation of fluency scores for these students, with an overall mean of 76.75 WCPM and a standard deviation of 28.22. Their WCPM scores ranged from 11 to 144! Obviously, it is quite possible to be a highly skilled decoder out of context and yet be a less fluent reader. In fact, only 25 percent of the high-scoring decoders achieved a fluency rate of 90 WCPM and above while reading literature, the benchmark for highly fluent second grade readers according to many fluency researchers and assessments (Good and Kaminski 2002; Shinn et al. 1992).

When we looked at the students with phonics scores in the lowest 25th percentile, we found an even weaker relationship to fluency. There was no correlation, not even a mild one, between their phonics and fluency scores. The mean of their fluency scores was 55.26 WCPM with a standard deviation of 21.89. Although their mean is lower than that of the high phonics group, their WCPM scores varied widely too, ranging from 30 to 104. Obviously, it is also possible to be a poor decoder and still read somewhat fluently or even very fluently. This means that we just can't know for sure that a student who performs poorly on isolated phonics tasks will also be unable to read fluently when reading authentic texts.

In terms of classroom literacy practice, our findings clearly indicate that we need to use caution in assuming that improving students' skill in sounding out words through more intensive phonics instruction will necessarily result in faster, more accurate reading (if that's your goal). Some students will be able to read literature fluently without being expert decoders out of context. These kids should not be held back from reading real books until they can expertly decode out of context. Other students will be expert decoders out of context but read with minimal fluency. More phonics instruction may not improve their fluency.

Turning to theoretical issues, these results challenge the strong claims that decoding is a prerequisite of fluency. Our research findings suggest that while decoding skill may co-occur to some degree with fluency across large research populations, a strong directionality or causal relationship between them cannot be assumed. Other factors may have stronger effects on reading fluency than the ability to decode words. The strong variability of decoding skill in fluent readers and of fluency rates in strong decoders propels us to look for other ways to understand the nature of fluency beyond the simplistic notion of rapid or automatic decoding. We turn now to an exploration of those possibilities.

The ability to decode print out of context transfers to the high use of graphophonic cues in the context of reading and consequently to greater fluency.

Perhaps, as you've read this chapter so far, you may be wondering whether the fluency with which readers read a text has more to do with how they are decoding the words *in that particular text*, than how they decode a set of pseudo words out of context. Does a reader's ability to sound out letters and letter patterns out of context (the litmus test for phonic skill according to subscribers to the automaticity model of reading) necessarily transfer to the reading of authentic literature? If so, does a greater use of graphophonic cues in text words account for the fluency with which a reader reads that text?

To begin answering these questions, we analyzed the variables from our miscue analysis data reflecting use of graphophonic cues in relation to the pseudo word phonics test scores to see whether there was a relationship between the two. Surprisingly, we found only a weak relationship between phonics scores and two of the six graphophonic variables: a weak but significant *negative* correlation between SOME sound similarity (r=−.43) and SOME graphic similarity (r=−.19). There was no correlation between the phonics scores and HIGH sound similarity or NO graphic or sound similarity. This means that for the students in our study, on the whole, their skill in decoding letters and letter patterns into sounds out of context has little or no relationship to how they use graphophonic cues in context. In fact, the higher the phonics scores, the lower the use of SOME graphophonic cues.

To confirm this finding, we looked again at the students with phonics scores ranked in the highest and lowest 25th percentiles to compare their use of graphophonic cues. We found that the top group's mean on SOME use of sound cues was half that of the low group, but their means for HIGH and NO graphic and sound similarity were almost the same. Basically, this means that students with the highest and lowest phonics percentiles used graphophonic cues similarly when they were actually reading stories, with the exception of high decoders who made less use of SOME sound cues. This seems rather counterintuitive, especially given the accepted wisdom about the value of teaching phonics outside of meaningful contexts. Why are we drilling kids in isolated phonics tasks when this skill doesn't transfer over to authentic reading? It might even be counterproductive to do so, given that the miscues of the highest decoders out of context reflected less use of SOME sound cues of words in context.

Now we'll turn to the question of whether or not the use of graphophonic cues in context was related to the rate and accuracy with which our students read the stories. To answer this question we looked at the graphophonic variables from the miscue analysis in relation to the WCPM, or fluency scores, for the stories. Again we found no correlation between any of the graphophonic variables and the fluency scores with the exception of a weak but significant *negative* relationship to SOME use of sound cues (r=−.27). This means that, on the whole, the more rapid and accurate readers are not distinguishable from the less accurate, slower readers in terms of their use of graphophonic cues. In fact, their means for NO use and HIGH use of graphic and sound cues are almost identical (64.50 for the high fluency group versus 66.37 for the low group on HIGH sound similarity; 73.87 for the high fluency group versus 73.85 for the low group on HIGH graphic similarity).

At this point we can confidently challenge the assumption that the ability to decode print out of context transfers to the high use of graphophonic cues in the context of reading and consequently to greater fluency. We do not find sufficient evidence that students who decode successfully out of context transfer that skill to the use of graphophonic cues in context, nor do we find any evidence that their use of graphophonic cues in context relates to their reading rate and accuracy as measured by the gold standard of correctly read words per minute. The notion that decoding is key to fluency must be reassessed.

The ability to comprehend text is dependent upon a high level of decoding skill in and out of context.

We will now examine a claim that is foundational to the recommendations of the National Reading Panel Report and embedded into the Reading First provisions of No Child Left Behind: strong decoding skills in and out of context of reading is foundational to achieving higher levels of comprehension. Chapter 5 explores the relationship between fluency and comprehension; here we would like to look at whether our data suggests a strong relationship of the phonic and graphophonic variables to the variables of meaning construction and retelling. Do students with stronger comprehension have higher phonics scores? Do they make greater use of graphophonic cues during reading? Just what seems to be the relationship between decoding and comprehension?

To investigate these questions we ran a correlation between the phonic and graphophonic variables and the meaning construction and retelling variables. We found that there was a weak but significant relationship (r=.36) between NO LOSS of meaning for the miscues that readers produced and their phonics percentile scores. This suggests a slight tendency for students with greater meaning construction during reading to have better phonics scores out of context and vice versa. Looking more closely at the students with the highest and lowest phonics percentiles, however, we don't see a large difference in means for NO LOSS of meaning construction; the high and low phonics groups had means of 43.50 and 35.6 respectively on NO LOSS of meaning. Each group also had a very large range of NO LOSS of meaning scores, ranging from 8 percent to 84 percent for the high phonics group, and 4 percent to 85 percent for the low phonics group. This is reflective of the weak correlation found between the phonics and meaning construction found for the entire data set.

When we turn to the relationship between meaning and the use of graphophonic cues within the reading of a story, we see an even weaker relationship, but this time in the opposite direction. There was a significant, weak correlation between NO LOSS of meaning and SOME sound similarity (r=–.30) and a significant but weak, positive correlation with NO sound similarity. This may be interpreted to mean that the students who are more apt to make miscues that do not disrupt meaning are also slightly less likely to use graphophonic cues during reading. In all, our findings suggest that we cannot assume that more meaningful reading reflects higher levels of decoding skill, either in or out of context. In fact, there is some indication that more meaningful readers are depending less on graphophonic cues. This cannot be attributed to a highly developed decoding skill that permits readers to shift attention to meaning instead of graphophonics (as the automaticity theorists claim) because there is no evidence that there is a strong relationship between phonics and graphophonics, nor phonics and meaning. We therefore must look beyond decoding as foundational to meaning constructing during reading.

As explained in Chapter 5, it is useful to distinguish between meaning construction during reading or comprehending and overall comprehension at completion of the reading. In miscue analysis research we assess comprehension through obtaining retellings from readers when they are finished reading. As previously discussed, this retelling is open-ended and consists of an unaided retelling and an aided retelling during which the researcher or teacher follows up with spontaneous questions relevant to what the reader has already retold. The previous discussion provided our results for comprehending, but what did we learn about the relationship of phonics and graphophonics to comprehension?

What we learned is quite simple to state: there is virtually no positive relationship between comprehension and students' decoding skills out of context or their use of graphophonics in context. If anything, there is a slight adverse relationship ($r=-.31$) between decoding and retelling, suggesting a slight tendency for students with better comprehension to be poorer decoders (at least on this pseudo word test).

When we consider the findings for both meaning construction during reading and comprehension after reading, it becomes clear that we cannot accept the widely held and federally promulgated claim that the ability to comprehend text is dependent upon a high level of decoding skill in and out of context. For the young readers in our study this is simply not the case. Furthermore, we also need to reject the final claim on our list: Highly competent decoders are better able to read with comprehension. In fact, the group with the highest phonics scores, ranking 75th percentile and above in relation to the national norm, actually had a somewhat lower mean retelling score (50.72) than the group who ranked at the 25th percentile and below on their phonics scores (63.39).

Contrary to the line fed to parents and educators through the media, and contrary to the rationale for the mandates of Reading First, we found only a vague, and possibly adverse, relationship between decoding and comprehension. If reading for meaning and comprehending is really the goal we set for our children, then perhaps it's time to look elsewhere for strategies to achieve this. Though we would not claim that graphophonics is of no value to readers as one of several cueing systems that can be used to efficiently construct meaning, perhaps it is time to topple decoding from its throne as the royal cure for all our reading ills.

Phonics Versus Literature Programs
What's the Difference?

As discussed in Chapter 3, a direct result of the National Reading Panel (NRP) Report and the subsequent No Child Left Behind (NCLB) Act of 2001 is that many teachers throughout the country have been mandated to teach reading using one of the commercial phonics programs that meets with Reading First requirements. This means that in order for a state to receive federal dollars, they must adopt a program that reflects five fundamental components of reading instruction as outlined in the NRP Report: phonemic awareness, phonics, vocabulary, fluency, and comprehension. Furthermore, these programs must demonstrate that they are approaching phonics through direct, systematic instruction, presumably because it leads to automatic and rapid decoding results and, in turn, fluency and comprehension. Naturally, most commercial programs now claim to be in compliance with Reading First requirements concerning systematic, explicit phonics and the "scientific research" that backs up their claims of effectiveness.

Two of the programs we studied in our research, Open Court and SRA Reading Mastery, are among the most widely adopted of such programs in the country. Both are published by the McGraw-Hill Company. The websites promoting each of these programs boldly assert that they are scientifically-based, align exquisitely with Reading First requirements (meaning they systematically and directly teach each component of reading), and are wildly successful in raising student reading levels as evidenced by standardized test scores. They offer "research evidence" of their success by referencing and quoting studies that demonstrate dramatic gains on either the Stanford 9 (or a state-adapted version thereof) or the TerraNova CTBS (also produced by McGraw-Hill).

When one looks at McGraw-Hill's "research evidence" more closely, however, alarm bells start ringing. First, most of the research studies presented by McGraw-Hill as evidence of the success of SRA Reading Mastery and Open Court were conducted by publisher-funded researchers. This is like trusting studies conducted by a pharmaceutical company's own scientists on the effectiveness and safety of their medications without an outside review. When there are profits to be made, company sponsored research must be scrutinized with a microscope.

Second, and perhaps more importantly, elevated test scores are automatically presumed to be direct indicators of actual student growth in phonemic awareness and phonics skills, vocabulary, fluency, and comprehension. Even if one accepts these components as fundamental to reading, we have no way of knowing if performance on standardized tests, especially those produced by the program publishers themselves, is a result of test coaching and instructional alignment or real-world increases in reading ability. In other words, the most critical question is never answered: Do these programs increase students' ability to read progressively more sophisticated materials with greater fluency and comprehension?

This is precisely the litmus test we conducted. We asked whether, after two years of implementation, the two phonics-based programs in our study, SRA Reading Mastery and Open Court, resulted in greater fluency (at least in terms of accuracy and rate), comprehension, and strategy use than the guided reading and literature-based programs when students read real literature. We believe that this raises the bar for evidenced-based claims of effectiveness. After all, if programs produce students who only read better on tests and not real-world reading material, then what evidence for effectiveness is that? Should precious education dollars be spent on expensive commercial phonics-based programs if we see no real-world benefit to readers?

What follows is a discussion of our findings regarding these very important questions. More specifically, we will examine whether the two phonics-based programs outperformed the literature-based and guided reading programs by resulting in more fluent reading (putting aside the question of its importance in reading), greater use of graphophonics and other cueing systems, greater ability to construct meaning during reading, and better overall comprehension of the story as evidenced by retellings.

Do phonics programs produce more fluent readers than literature-based programs?

As explained in Chapter 4, we developed several measures of accuracy and rate in order to study the claims that have often been made about the importance of these variables in the reading process. We have already shown that claims about the correlational or prerequisite relationships between fast, accurate reading and comprehension have not, on the whole, been borne out by the data derived from reading of authentic literature by the second graders in our research. Using the same data from the four program sites, we will now examine the claims made in the NRP report and by the publishers of commercial reading programs that an instructional diet of direct systematic phonics instruction is necessary for the development of fluent reading (fast, accurate reading), and thus better comprehension. If this is true, we should see a statistically significant difference between the Open Court and SRA Reading Mastery programs and the literature-based and guided reading programs on fluency variables, other miscue analysis variables, the retellings, and the phonics test.

When comparing the four programs in terms of the number of words read correctly in the first minute (WCPM) (the gold standard used for many fluency tests), we found that there were no statistically significant differences among the four programs. In other words, we found that the phonics programs did not produce readers that read both more accurately and quickly in the first minute of their reading of real literature. It should be noted that we collected this data from students *before* the imposition of the DIBELS assessment on classrooms. So this and other findings do not reflect variations in fluency test coaching, but rather results of programmatic instruction. When we looked across the reading of the whole text and just the portion analyzed for miscues, there were still no significant differences among the four programs in reading rate or accuracy. For each program there was a wide variation in the rate at which students read the stories and in the number of miscues they made, but overall, the two phonics programs did not produce more fluent readers according to any of our measures.

These findings are significant for practical as well as theoretical reasons. First, they challenge the publishers' claims that intensive, systematic phonics programs are requisite for building fast and accurate text reading in the real-world sense. We found no justification for requiring teachers to use heavily prescribed or scripted commercial programs for the purpose of uniformly producing fluent readers.

Despite the fact that there were no significant fluency differences among the phonics-based and literature-based schools, we were still interested in learning whether there might be differences in the factors affecting students' fluency in the different types of programs. Which variables seem to correlate with reading rate and accuracy in phonics-based and literature-based schools?

We found that for the students in our two phonics programs there was a tendency (not significant) toward an inverse relationship between retelling and fluency. This suggests that, for many readers, reading for meaning slowed them down or reading faster and more accurately hurt their comprehension. Given that correlation cannot assume causality, all we can say for sure is that there is no indication that systematic phonics programs lead students to read faster or more accurately. Those who do read more quickly and accurately do not necessarily comprehend any better than slower readers; perhaps some even comprehend less.

Some might argue that these findings may be expected in second grade, given that both Open Court and SRA Reading Mastery deliberately focus more on phonics and less on comprehension in the primary years. The rationale for this emphasis on phonics is based on the assumption that fluency is achieved through rapid and automatic decoding of words during reading, resulting ultimately in comprehension. If this assumption is correct, we should see a significant correlation between readers' use of phonic information and our measures of fluency. This also turned out not to be the case.

We found no relationship between any graphophonic variable during reading and any measures of rate and accuracy for the students in phonics-based programs. This suggests that for two of the most widely used commercial programs that claim to be "scientifically based," intensive systematic phonics instruction did not produce readers who read faster, more accurately or with better comprehension.

Turning to the literature-based programs we can report somewhat similar results. While we found no relationship between use of graphophonics and rapid, accurate reading for these students either, data suggests an inverse relationship between use of graphophonics and reading rate alone. The number of words read per minute for the story (reading rate) correlated negatively with HIGH use of graphophonics, and positively with NO use of graphophonics. This suggests that the more rapid readers in the literature-based programs tend not to rely heavily upon graphophonic information during reading. Instead we found that these students were focused more on constructing meaning and comprehending. In fact, we found significant positive correlations between NO LOSS of meaning and the rate and accuracy for the first minute of reading as well as for the entire story. For one of these literature-based programs, there was also a significant correlation between retelling and all the fluency measures, indicating that the readers with better comprehension read more fluently.

What does all this mean for the theory and practice of reading? It means that when looking at students reading real literature, we find no justification for the assumption that fluency can only be achieved through rapid and automatic decoding taught with systematic, intensive phonics instruction. We also must challenge the assumption that more accurate and rapid reading resulting from such intensive phonics instruction leads to better comprehension. Remember that fluency was not related to high use of graphophonics or to comprehension for the students in the Open Court and SRA Reading Mastery programs. We can only infer that fast and accurate readers in phonics programs must be word calling through some (not high) use of letter or sound cues and without regard to making sense of the story. Perhaps this is a consequence of reading decodable texts that lack substance or teaching phonics and skills removed from the context of meaningful reading.

To illustrate these results, let's look closer at the reading of students in phonics- and literature-based programs. Figure 7–1 illustrates the miscues of a more fluent reader in a phonics-based program.

Notice that the miscues of this reader look or sound somewhat like the words in the text, but do not make sense in the sentence. Notice also that the reader does not take the time to go back and correct the miscues so that they will make more sense. Readers like this may read more rapidly because they are not taking the time to construct or monitor meaning. In fact, we found a significant difference between the phonics- and literature-based programs in relation to self-correction strategies. Readers from the phonics programs make significantly fewer

Jamaica turned to see if (Berto) was still there. He stood

washington
watching. Then (he) tried to (step) over the (ditch) and his foot

washed
smashed the wall. ....

pushed
(“Berto,”) the woman pushing the stroller (said) “leave this (girl)

along
alone.

FIGURE 7–1. *A fluent reader in phonics-based program*

anybody
In fact he liked anyone who was nice to Mario. But

it was late now: time to crawl back to his

(uc)
2. nice
1. nice
comfortable (niche in the wall to go to sleep ...

the subway's
He had heard the rumble of subway trains
                              ^

(c) *their*   *from*   *that*
and the shriek their iron wheels make
                          ^   ^

corners
when they go around a corner.

FIGURE 7–2. *A fluent reader in a literature-based program*

attempts to correct their miscues both successfully and unsuccessfully. These readers either don't notice or don't think it's important to reconsider what they are reading when it doesn't makes sense. In contrast, let's look at a more fluent reader from a literature-based program (see Figure 7–2).

Like the previous student, this reader makes substitutions that do bear some graphophonic resemblance to the words in the text. But this reader also seems to be predicting and monitoring meaning. We see that for the miscues that do not make sense in the sentence the reader at least tries to correct them by making several alternative attempts, and for some miscues, corrects successfully. It is important to note that for some of the readers in the literature-based programs, these meaning-monitoring correction strategies did slow their reading rate. But one must ask, as we do elsewhere in this book, are we willing to sacrifice meaning for speed and accuracy?

Are there any other differences between students in phonics-based versus literature-based programs in their reading of authentic literature?

Besides the issue of fluency, we were also interested in whether there were any pronounced differences among the phonics-based and literature-based programs in relation to students' overall focus on comprehending, comprehension, use of graphophonics, or reading strategies. Finding no significant differences among the programs in terms of the students' fluency levels, we examined whether there were any other benefits of phonics-based instruction that might justify the shunning of literature-based programs as is now taking place as a result of current federal reading policy. Should teachers abandon literature-based reading instruction, including embedded phonics (as the proponents of Reading First would have them do), in favor of commercial systematic phonics and skills instruction? Will such phonics programs, despite skepticism on the part of holistic-oriented educators, result in better decoding, comprehension, and strategic processing? Using our original data base of over one hundred students, we felt we were well-positioned to begin answering these questions and scrutinizing the NRP claims and NCLB policies that have so radically changed the way reading is taught in our classrooms.

Phonics and Graphophonics

In Chapter 6, we reported that we found no positive relationship between phonics and graphophonic use and any of the comprehending or comprehension variables. But this did not answer the question regarding whether there were significant differences in phonics use among the students in the phonics-based and literature-based programs. Programs such as Open Court and SRA Reading Mastery have supposedly gained federal support precisely because they claim to help students achieve phonics knowledge earlier and more effectively than literature-based programs. Does this hold true for the children in our study?

Our research design permitted us to assess students' ability to decode out of context by using the Woodcock Johnson Psycho-Educational Battery-R (WJPE-R) Word Attack subtest (Woodcock and Bonner Johnson 1990) and to assess students' use of graphophonic cues during the reading of the literature (by using miscue analysis). We were quite surprised by the results. There were no significant differences among students in the four programs on any one of our measures of phonics use. Despite two years of intensive phonics instruction, the students in the Open Court and SRA Reading Mastery programs did not significantly outperform the students in either of the two literature-based programs in their decoding of pseudo words on the Woodcock Johnson subtest. Furthermore, the students in the phonics-based program did not use graphophonic cues to a significantly greater extent than those in the literature-based programs.

We can conclude from this (and you can inform your administrators and parents) that, at least according to our research, after almost two years of intensive, systematic phonics instruction using two of the most widely mandated commercial phonics programs, there is no evidence of superiority in students' use of phonics for isolated decoding or in the use of graphophonic cues in the context of reading real literature. That means that contrary to NRP and Reading First claims, literature-based programs such as those we studied support the development of phonic knowledge just as well by the end of second grade.

Meaning Construction and Comprehension

When we compared all of the students in the phonics-based programs with all those in the literature programs, we found a striking difference in their focus on meaning during reading. The phonics-based group had a significantly higher percentage of miscues that resulted in a loss of meaning. When you combine this finding with those previously reported concerning their significantly fewer attempts to correct successfully, or even unsuccessfully, the picture that emerges is that these readers were significantly more likely to make miscues that made no sense and weren't corrected.

Based on our findings, we can assert that phonics-based instruction is significantly less likely than literature-based instruction to lead to reading that focuses on meaning construction. Literature-based readers seem to at least try to make sense of what they are reading and attempt to correct when they aren't successful. No wonder that the literature-based group also had a higher average retelling score than the phonics-based students, though this was not quite significant. According to research conducted by our colleagues with the same data set (Martens et al. 2005), the literature-based students demonstrated a deeper level of understanding as evidenced by their inferences, connections, and ability to formulate a theme for the stories they read. The phonics-based students tended to simply relate the events in the stories without deeper interpretation.

Conclusion

What have we learned from our study regarding the impact of phonics- versus literature-based programs by the end of second grade after almost two years of instruction? Do phonics-based programs have clear advantages over literature-based programs as claimed by commercial publishers and asserted in Reading First? Based on our findings for over one hundred children, matched demographically and taught by competent teachers using two of the most widely used phonics-based programs, we must answer no to both these questions.

In fact we find quite the opposite.

Students in phonics-based programs:
- do not read more fluently (faster and more accurately)
- are more likely to word call in order to read faster
- are not more highly skilled at decoding words out of context
- do not make greater use of graphophonic cues while reading

- are less likely to focus on meaning while reading
- are less likely to attempt self-correction when their reading does not make sense
- may be less able to comprehend what they read with depth

Again, these findings don't apply to every student in our phonics-based programs. There are indeed students in these programs who read with fluency, meaning, and comprehension. There are also students in the literature-based programs we studied who read with little meaning construction and comprehension. There was a great deal of variation among the students in each group. Nevertheless, our findings can contribute to public and school-level discussions as to whether there is sufficient justification for federal policies that all but eliminate literature-based, meaning-centered programs for federal funding. Our findings challenge the wisdom of pouring millions of dollars into commercial programs that straitjacket teachers with detailed instructions or scripts and reduce children's access to high quality literature in their classrooms. At the very least, it is clear that further research is needed to investigate these critical issues in reading instruction and national reading policies.

Does Fluency Distinguish Between More and Less Proficient Readers?

In the previous chapter we reported our finding that intensive, systematic phonics programs did not produce readers with higher levels of rate and accuracy than did the literature-based programs. We also found, however, that for students who learned to read using literature-based programs, there was a relationship between the fluency with which they read and their construction of meaning. This was not the case for the students in the phonics-based programs, for whom reading faster and more accurately was not related to meaning. Perhaps both sets of students learned well what their programs taught: in the phonics-based programs better reading equals faster and more accurate reading, regardless of comprehension, whereas in the literature-based programs better reading means greater use of multiple cues to more easily predict and monitor meaning construction.

We see, then, that in both these types of programs, the underlying definition of reading frames the literacy practices in the classrooms and does indeed influence students' reading processes. We would also expect that the contrasting models for what constitutes a better reader underlies how students' reading levels are determined. If so, then classrooms would differ considerably in terms of which aspects of reading are key for evaluating students' reading levels. In more and more classrooms, the key factor used to determine reading level is fluency, operationalized as rate and accuracy. But is fluency really the distinctive feature that distinguishes between more and less able reading?

If, as the National Reading Panel Report and Reading First purport, fluency is one of the main pillars of successful reading, then the answer would be yes. In terms of our study, that would mean finding a significant difference between the more and less proficient readers in measures of accuracy and rate. But our dilemma in pursuing this analysis is figuring out how to identify more and less able readers independent of fluency. To solve this problem, we decided to address our question using three different lenses for grouping our students based on their "abilities." First, we used the groupings that the teachers identified for us as high, middle, and low readers. Second, we used the book levels that the students read, assuming that the higher the level books (according to Fountas and Pinnell 2000) students could read, the better readers they were. Third, we grouped students using the notion of reading proficiency which regards better readers as those who get the most meaning from what they read. For each of these grouping procedures, we examined whether fluency is a key distinguishing factor between readers of differing reading abilities. In other words, do the more able readers in each condition read more accurately and quickly?

Comparing Identified Levels of Readers

You may recall that in the original collection of data we asked the teachers in each program to identify the high, middle, and lower readers in their classes without interfering in the identification process. We learned from our interviews that decisions of teachers in the phonics-based classrooms were informed by the program assessments and standardized testing. Teachers in the literature-based classrooms identified different levels of readers based upon individual informal assessments, including Running Records. We then used selection criteria described earlier to choose ten children of each level at each site to include in our study. For this follow-up study of fluency, we had access to a slightly reduced subset of students from the original study. Fortunately, however, we still had a very close match in the number of students assigned to each level for both the phonics- and literature-based programs.

As teachers, teacher educators, and researchers we have often wondered if students who are divided into different ability groups in classrooms are really reading differently from one another in significant ways. This is a very important question because the ability group students are assigned to seriously affects their future literacy instruction, as well as their self-esteem and, perhaps, motivation. In some programs it is difficult for students to move up to a higher group once they have been assigned to the low group. We need to be quite sure that if we group by ability we are using criteria that are well supported by research and experience.

Was fluency a key criterion used by the teachers in our study (perhaps intuitively) to identify the students as high, middle, and low readers? If so, does fluency distinguish the students in any other important ways, such as their ability to comprehend what they are reading? Or are the students grouped only on the basis of whether they are perceived to read faster or slower, more accurately or less accurately? To answer these questions we examined our miscue analysis data to determine whether there were any significant differences on our fluency variables among the groups of students identified as high, middle, and low readers in the programs and in the literature-based programs.

What we found was very interesting and provides insight into whether fluency is, and if it should be, used as a criterion for distinguishing among ability groups. For the two phonics programs, we found that there indeed was a significant difference among the teacher-identified groups on our fluency measures. That means that whether they were aware of it or not, the grouping practices used by the teachers at these schools were based primarily on the rate and accuracy of the readers. This makes sense given the focus of instruction and operating definition of reading. Nevertheless, this was not an entirely useful criterion to use, because we only found significant differences in fluency between the lowest and the highest readers. There were no significant differences on our fluency variables between the high and middle groups, nor between the low and middle groups. What this means is that rate and accuracy distinguishes between only the highest and lowest readers in the classroom; it isn't helpful in distinguishing among those groups and the students who are considered middle level readers. Some of those middle readers probably read with rate and accuracy comparable to those either considered high readers or low readers. This is worrisome to us as teachers because in real-life terms some of those readers in the middle level may be misplaced and receiving instruction and materials that are either above or below their actual ability.

What is even more concerning is that the students in the three groups are not distinguishable in many other important ways. There are absolutely no significant differences among these groups in their construction of meaning during reading, nor their retellings after reading.

They aren't even distinguishable on the basis of how much they use graphophonic information during reading. The only other aspects of reading that distinguish the high readers from the low readers are their use of grammatical structure (for example, substituting a noun for a noun, a verb for a verb, etc.) and their scores on the phonics test. We found that fluency as a criterion for determining reading levels in programs does not reflect anything else about readers besides their ability to decode nonwords in isolation and attend to grammatical cues. It says nothing about their ability to construct meaning, monitor meaning, or comprehend what they read. Is fluency alone, then, a worthwhile criterion for ability grouping our students?

Let's turn now to the literature-based programs to determine what distinguishes among these high, middle, and low readers as identified by their teachers. It is important to note that there were no fixed ability groupings in the literature-based classrooms we studied. The students were flexibly grouped and regrouped periodically for guided reading lessons. Nevertheless, the teachers could easily divide the class into high, middle, and low readers for the purpose of our study. Do these groups of readers also vary significantly on our fluency variables? Were there any other aspects of reading that distinguished the readers in these groups? We put our data to the test.

Like the phonics programs, we found that there was a significant difference on the fluency variables for readers of different levels in the literature-based programs. But these differences were between the high readers and both the low and middle readers. There was no significant difference in fluency between the middle and low readers. This means that fluency was only useful as a criterion for distinguishing between the highest readers and all the other readers in the class. The middle and low readers' rate and accuracy scores were statistically indistinguishable from one another. The identified high readers were also significantly stronger than were all the rest of the readers in their use of grammatical cues and some (not high) use of sound cues.

One clue as to why high readers in the literature-based programs have a significantly higher reading rate than the other readers may be our finding on unsuccessful corrections. The low and middle readers had a significantly higher percentage of unsuccessful attempts to correct their miscues. Stopping to reread and make multiple attempts to correct their miscues surely slows down their rates. Teachers' decisions about the reading levels of their students may be an intuitive response to this frequent disruption in the overall flow of reading, especially if these disruptions affect meaning construction. Is this the case? Based upon our analyses we would have to answer this question with a yes. It turns out that there is a significant difference between the groups on our meaning construction variables. The low group's miscues result in loss of meaning significantly more often than do the high group's miscues. Conversely, the high group's miscues result in no loss of meaning significantly more often than do the miscues of the rest of the students. Simply stated, for the literature-based programs, students identified by their teachers as high readers make more sense when they read than the other readers. This is in stark contrast to the high, middle, and low groups in the phonics-based programs who do not differ significantly in terms of making sense when they read.

One way to interpret these findings is that in phonics-based programs, the operational definition of reading places a heavier value on reading fast and accurately, even if it is detrimental to meaning construction. In literature-based programs, the operational definition of reading places value on rate and accuracy in so much as it reflects disruptions to the flow and meaning construction while reading. Though teachers in both programs consider fluency as a distinctive characteristic of successful reading, they do so for different reasons and goals. Automaticity of reading is the goal of the phonics-based programs. Making sense is the goal of reading in the literature-based programs, and fluency (fewer disruptions) may help readers achieve this goal.

Book Level

Another way we can examine the role of fluency in successful reading is to compare the miscues and retellings of children who read books at different levels of complexity for our study. As previously discussed, we identified three books at eight different levels according to Fountas and Pinnell's (2000) book leveling. This gave us a book gradient that went from simple picture books, such as *Happy Birthday, Sam* (Hutchins 1978) to the first chapter of *Cricket in Times Square* (Selden 1960). Given that the students in our study were matched to books that were as close as possible to their "instructional" level (challenging, but not beyond their reach), we assumed that the students who read the more complex texts were more accomplished readers than those who read the easy picture books. This provided us an opportunity to test the assumption that fluency is a key component of successful reading, and to test the usefulness of fluency measures for distinguishing among readers of varying reading abilities. In terms of the students in our study, we wondered if readers of increasingly more complex texts have corresponding increases in measures of rate and accuracy.

Our initial findings indicated a positive correlation between fluency measures and book levels, meaning that readers of higher level books tended to read faster and more accurately. Without further analysis, these findings seemed to support the assumption that fluency is indeed a key characteristic of higher reading ability and could justifiably be used to assess and group readers. But then we looked a bit more deeply to determine if this correlation reflected an incremental increase with each higher book level. This would be important to know, since teachers are being mandated to use fluency to level and group children fairly precisely.

What we found should be taken seriously by proponents of this practice. It seems that our measures of fluency did not increase incrementally from book level to book level. We only found a significant difference in fluency between the readers of the highest level book (the chapter book) and the lower level books (picture books). There were no significant differences in fluency measures among the readers of book levels 6, 7, and 8, nor among readers of book levels 1, 2, 3, 4, and 5. So, instead of finding a step-by-step increase in students' fluency from book level to book level, we found that fluency scores for readers across a large range of books were not significantly different from one another. Furthermore, we found that our fluency variables, especially words correct per minute (WCPM), did not even predict the correct book level order. In other words, if we used just WCPM to determine reading ability we would incorrectly conclude that the students who read book 6 were somewhat higher readers than the students who read book 7, and that the students who read level 3 books were somewhat better readers than those who read level 4 and equal to those who read level 6.

One other interesting finding was that even our most fluent and accomplished readers who read the first chapter of a children's novel in second grade with comprehension would not meet the benchmark for fluency identified by any number of scales (Good and Kaminski 2002;

Hasbrouck and Tindall 2006; Shanahan 2006). By DIBELS standards the group of level 8 readers who read an average of 83 WCPM would be considered "At Some Risk." When assessment results are in direct contradiction to common sense and our professional judgment as teachers, we must question their validity. Though we acknowledge that fluency did distinguish between readers of a chapter book and readers of the simplest picture books, we wonder who among us wouldn't realize that on his or her own. We don't know of a teacher who would miss that great a difference in reading ability! Fluency scores would not help teachers to make finer distinctions among readers, and worse, could cause them to misjudge and misplace students.

So far, the findings for this part of our study suggest that whatever researchers have found regarding the value of fluency measures for predicting test scores does not apply to predicting the ability to read real books, except at a very crude level. But we still have another way to examine the role of fluency in reading and its assumed importance as a component of successful reading. For this we look through our third lens—that of reading proficiency.

Reading Proficiency

In our view, reading proficiency involves effective and efficient reading (Goodman 2004). Effective reading refers to the successful construction of meaning during reading and overall comprehension of the text. Comprehension is the result of a transaction that occurs between a particular reader and a text within a given social context. In this view, comprehension does not assume a fixed *correct* meaning that a reader *derives* from the text. Readers draw upon their experiences, background knowledge, purpose, interpretation of the task, and many other factors to construct a personally meaningful and relevant understanding of what they have read.

Proficient reading also requires efficiency. This term does not refer to a fixed speed and accuracy of reading, but rather the flexibility that permits readers to change their rate appropriately as they think and construct meaning for a given text. Flurkey (1998) found that proficient readers who are both effective and efficient tend to vary their speed as they read a single text in direct response to the task of making sense. He calls the speeding up and slowing down during reading *flow* rather than fluency. Flow reflects his finding that there isn't actually a fixed and consistent rate of speed that readers exhibit throughout the reading of a text, or even a paragraph or clause. Proficient and nonproficient reading alike exhibit this variation in flow, but the variations of proficient reading are not quite as dramatic. Peaks and valleys of proficient reading are less likely to be punctuated by frequent very long pauses or repeated regressions or multiple attempts to correct a miscue, all of which may disrupt the processing of meaning, or effectiveness. Less proficient reading exhibits more dramatic peaks and valleys read at an overall slower pace. (Flurkey 1998) and does impact or reflect difficulty in constructing meaning.

It is important to point out that not all effective reading is efficient. We all know children and adults who comprehend well, but are slow readers. In fact, we all experience this at times depending on what and why we are reading. We might understand the written directions to assemble something but have to read it slowly, rereading sections, regressing often, pausing to think, and even reading aloud while pointing to the print. In this case the reading is effective, but not as efficient as we might like. The reverse is also true. We have all experienced reading something quickly, perhaps on a timed test, and realizing that we haven't fully or deeply comprehended. Children who think reading well is reading fast may also experience this reduced level of understanding.

Again, we turn to our data to see whether fixed rates of fluency reflected in WCPM and our other measures are valuable in predicting effective reading as measured by meaning constructing variables and retellings. Will fluency, in the more common view of rate and accuracy, be predictive of effective reading? Will more effective reading result in higher fluency rates? Or does Flurkey's notion of flow more accurately describe our findings?

To address these questions we divided our readers in a number of ways. First we identified the top quartile of students in our study who were the fastest and most accurate readers based on WCPM. Then we identified the lowest quartile of students in our study based on WCPM, or the slowest and least accurate readers in the study. We examined these students to discover if we could predict, based upon this fluency measure, who were the most effective readers. We then identified the most and least effective readers, based upon measures of NO LOSS of meaning and retellings. Did the most effective readers have higher overall WCPM scores? Did the least effective readers have lower overall WCPM scores?

First we will consider the validity of using WCPM for distinguishing among the most and least effective readers. We found that there was a great deal of overlap among the most and least fluent readers on measures of reading effectiveness. In both groups, the range in reading effectiveness was very large. For the students with the highest fluency rates, their scores on NO LOSS of meaning (or the percentage of miscues that did not disrupt meaning) ranged from 24 percent to 85 percent. Their retelling scores ranged from 27 percent to 88 percent. For the students with the lowest fluency rates, their percentage of miscues that did not disrupt meaning ranged from 8 percent to 68 percent. Their retelling scores ranged from 23 percent to 88 percent. Although the minimum and maximum effectiveness scores did correspond to the level of fluency one might expect, the overlap of scores was so great that many children would be misjudged if assessed using fluency rates alone.

When we compared the fluency rates of the most effective and least effective groups of readers in our study, we once again found a great deal of overlap. The range of WCPM for the most effective readers was 44 to 144. That is a full 100 WCPM difference! Clearly there are proficient readers in this group who are both effective and efficient in their reading of the text. But there are also those who are effective but not efficient; they understand what they are reading but with greater variation in their patterns of flow. The range of WCPM for the least effective readers was from 25 to 96. This means that within this group there are readers who are truly nonproficient in their reading of this text and would be correctly assessed as in need of additional support. But there are also ineffective readers in this same group who would be mistakenly identified as readers who are not in need of additional support, due to their high fluency rate (even above 90 WCPM!). These are the children who fall through the cracks with the current fluency assessment craze.

What do our findings suggest about the competing theories of fluency and the value of fluency for assessing reading ability? It suggests that we need to challenge the fluency-is-prerequisite-to-comprehension and fluency-equals-comprehension theories currently in vogue, and embrace the transactional model with a proficiency view of literacy. Our findings cast doubt on the claims of No Child Left Behind that fluency is a major component of reading that is prerequisite to comprehension. Apparently, there are many students whose fluency rates (as measured by WCPM) are on the lower end, but who are quite effective readers. Conversely, there are many students who read with higher fluency that are not effective readers and are unable to construct meaning and comprehend. Reading assessments based on benchmark fluency rates (especially when comprehension assessment is minimal or absent from the assessment instrument) are incapable of identifying which of the faster readers are actually proficient and which are not. Nor are they capable of distinguishing between slower readers who are effective readers and those who are not. Fluency simply casts too large a net, catching truly proficient readers as well as those who are fast but not effective. The net also catches truly ineffective, slower readers with those who are effective.

The only way to assess readers adequately is through the use of qualitative assessments by teachers who understand reading and understand their students. Teachers must have the opportunity to do more than count words with a stopwatch and place students in reading groups. We propose shifting our understanding of the role of rate and accuracy during reading to Flurkey's transactional notion of flow. Analyzing readers' variations in rate as well as their reading strategies and retelling can provide us with nuanced information regarding their proficiency (both effectiveness and efficiency) in reading a particular text. Once this type of information is ascertained by their teachers, students stand a much better chance of receiving instruction and reading opportunities that make sense for them. On the other hand, fluency as it is currently operationalized in the classroom can actually do our children more harm than good. It leaves too many readers, both proficient and non-proficient, behind.

What Does DIBELS Tell Us About Readers?

Every Friday after lunch Mrs. O'Brien has center time so that her second grade students can work together on various reading, writing, math, science, and problem-solving skills. This Friday five work stations are set up. All the students are busy either writing letters home describing what they learned in school this week, working with the tangram challenge cards, building simple machines with the K'Nex sets, or illustrating math word problems. Some are sitting at the kidney table with Mrs. O'Brien reading a story they will take home for the weekend to practice reading to their families. It's 1:30 pm, and Ms. Kim, the second grade paraprofessional, has just come in to complete the DIBELS (Dynamic Indicators of Basic Early Literacy Skills) benchmark assessments for the five students who need "intensive intervention and weekly monitoring." Joe, one of these five students, is working on his letter with Rodrick when Ms. Kim calls him to her desk in the corner of the room. Joe looks up when he hears his name, sags his shoulders, slowly rises out of his chair, and walks away from his friends, leaving his letter to his mother unfinished on the center table. He needs to complete his DIBELS test now.

Joe sits down at the testing desk and Ms. Kim says, "Joe, please read this out loud. If you get stuck, I will tell you the word so you can keep reading. When I say 'stop' I may ask you to tell me about what you read, so do your best reading. Start here. Begin" (Good and Kaminski 2002, 31–32). Ms. Kim immediately starts a stopwatch. Joe reads as fast as he can:

> If I had a robot, he would do everything I don't like to do. First, he'd brush his teeth. Then, he'd get dressed for school. I would stay in bed. . . . I would hug my dad and kiss my mom goodnight. My robot would have to hug my little brother. (Good and Kaminski 2002, Benchmark 3, 10)

Ms. Kim carefully follows the DIBELS Oral Reading Fluency directions, providing words for Joe when he pauses for more than three seconds. She marks each correct word Joe reads on her copy of the probe and stops Joe after one minute. She records Joe's score, and then asks him to tell her everything that he can remember about the passage. As Joe talks, Ms. Kim checks a boxed string of numbers under the passage counting the number of words as he talks, making sure he doesn't repeat anything and that all he talks about is in the probe he just read. Then she circles the total number of words in his response and sends him back to his seat.

By the time Joe gets back to his peers in his small group, it's time for the centers to change and Joe never finishes his letter. Mrs. O'Brien watches Joe, masking her discontent better than Joe, for she, like Joe, is disappointed. Mrs. O'Brien sees more value in Joe working together with Rodrick on his letter than she does in him being tested again on how fast he can read a DIBELS probe. But she has no power over this decision; it has become mandated district policy to follow the regimen prescribed in the DIBELS manual.

Scenes like this are repeated all over our nation. Children from preschool through third grade (and in some school districts well beyond) are monitored for weekly progress in what is being called basic early literacy skills. What is the motivation behind this practice? How has it come to be that testing has taken precedence over teaching? And that a program makes instructional decisions rather than a professional educator?

In previous chapters we presented evidence that the current popular practice of using fluency to group students for instruction is not justifiable. This practice overwhelmingly relies on the quantitative measures of rate and accuracy, and not on measures of meaning construction during the reading process or comprehension after reading. Because of the popularity of assessing young readers for exactly this purpose, however, we extended our research to include an investigation into the most commonly used assessment program, one the federal Reading First office strongly encourages states to include in their Reading First grant proposals: Dynamic Indicators of Basic Early Literacy Skills, Sixth Edition, or DIBELS (see *Reading First Program's Grant Application Process—Final Inspection Report* available at www.ed.gov/about /offices/list/oig/aireports/i13f0017.pdf).

Schools all over the United States have turned to DIBELS in an attempt to respond to the reading assessment mandates of No Child Left Behind. The DIBELS complete battery of tests includes these six assessments: Letter Naming Fluency, Initial Sound Fluency, Phoneme Segmentation Fluency, Nonsense Word Fluency, Oral Reading Fluency and Retell Fluency, and Word Use Fluency. Each DIBELS test is short, taking just one minute for each subset in the assessment program. According to the authors, Roland Good III and Ruth Kaminski, the individual assessments are designed to be "used to regularly monitor the development of early literacy and early reading skills" (www.dibels.org/dibels.html).

Good and Kaminski make strong claims regarding the usefulness of this assessment instrument in documenting reading progress and as a predictor of success on standardized tests. The program is also frequently used to group and level students for instruction as well as remediation. As we launched into our investigation of fluency, we were constantly nagged by more questions, questions specifically related to DIBELS Oral Reading Fluency, or DORF. Our original data set was collected before our state began widely implementing DIBELS. Given that DIBELS is so widespread and directly related to our research, we found it necessary to extend our study and try to determine whether DIBELS gives us any valuable information about early readers.

We started with a simple question: Are the time and money invested in DIBELS useful for classroom teachers? To answer this question, we needed to investigate how valuable the data collected for this assessment really is and if it can tell us anything about real reading. Would the claims made by Good and Kaminski hold true and provide adequate information regarding instructional decisions made for a group of readers like the ones in our larger study?

Our first step in seeking answers to these critical questions was to compare the rate of reading in the DORF assessment to our participants' reading rates of authentic children's literature. We reasoned that if a student's DORF was similar to his or her reading of authentic books (level-appropriate children's literature) the DORF may be a fair assessment of a student's oral reading fluency. We further reasoned that if oral reading rate and accuracy is a goal of instruction, and if we could find some consistency in oral reading behavior across texts, DORF may have some value in determining a student's instructional plan.

In addition, DIBELS claims to be able to make instructional recommendations for students based on their DORF. Since reading comprehension is the ultimate goal of any reading instruction, we wondered if we could find evidence to support DIBELS' instructional recommendations in areas of reading beyond oral reading proficiency, most notably, comprehension. In other words, would the instructional recommendations made by a DIBELS assessment support the levels of proficiency in any given student's reading comprehension? For this part of our inquiry we extended a study conducted by Martens, Arya, Wilson, and Jin (2005) investigating comprehension of second grade readers across multiple texts.

Using data gathered from thirteen second grade students, we asked the following formal research questions:

1. Does DORF provide us any important information in terms of rate and accuracy with which children read real books? In other words, what is the relationship of DIBELS measures of rate and accuracy (DORF) to rate and accuracy of reading trade books (words correct per minute, or WCPM)?
2. Is the instructional recommendation made by using DIBELS supported by the student's reading proficiency while reading real books?

In our earlier research we used four measures of rate and accuracy, WPM, WCPM, WPMmis, and WPMtext (see Chapter 4). Since we found a strong correlation between these measures, and because DORF is measured during the first minute of oral reading, only WCPM was used in our analysis. All data were collected at the end of the second grade year, and the students were asked to read and retell authentic children's books that were unfamiliar to them. The readings and retellings were audiotaped, miscues were coded, and retellings were scored according to miscue protocol.

Unlike the previous research, each student in this study (thirteen readers all in the same second grade class) engaged in more than one reading event; fifty-two total reading events comprise the data set. The participating students read either two or three of the following picture books: *Flossie and the Fox* (McKissack 1992); *Precious and the Boo Hag* (McKissack 2005); *Cherries and Cherry Pits* (Williams 1991); *A Letter to*

Amy (Keats 1998); *Peter's Chair* (Keats 1967), and *See You Tomorrow, Charles* (Cohen 1987). The school practiced homogeneous grouping at the grade level, and the students in this class were considered above grade level readers. Within the classroom, they were again separated into two groups by their teacher: one group was identified as high and the other as low. The more proficient readers, the high group, read three of the texts (*Flossie, Precious*, and *Cherries and Cherry Pits*) and the less proficient readers, the low group, read two texts (*Amy, Charles,* or *Peter*). Participants read only one book on any given day, with repeated interactions with researchers occurring over the course of several consecutive days. Researchers collected the data for the authentic literature reading following the same protocol used in the larger study (see Chapter 4).

The classroom teacher, trained by the school district to follow DIBELS protocol, collected the data for DORF. Students were asked to read a passage. The teacher timed the reading, stopping the student after one minute, and asked the student to retell what they remembered from the passage. The number of words read correctly was counted as the DORF score, and the number of relevant words spoken (no deviations, songs, or repetitions) in the retell was counted as the student spoke and recorded as the retelling fluency (RTF). This was repeated three times for each reader. The score recorded for the student was the middle score for each subtest. The highest and lowest DORF score, as well as the highest and lowest RTF scores, were not permanently recorded and were discarded.

DIBELS Retelling Fluency (RTF) is an optional part of the assessment program, and while the school collected RTF data on each participating student, in keeping with the choice given in the assessment program guide to make this test optional, the school personnel did not use the data to make instructional decisions. Therefore, the RTF scores will not be used in this examination of DIBELS and its relationship to authentic reading performance.

We were interested in viewing the group as a whole, much like teachers must do when planning group instruction. In addition, we were particularly interested in looking at individual readers, specifically examining the details of each student's reading behaviors similarly to how we would if we were the teacher charged with making individualized instructional decisions for each student. This required us to closely examine individual readers. When teachers focus intensely on students they often use methods that are similar to case study research (Merriam 1990). This is the methodology we employed, but we conducted a formal study as opposed to the somewhat informal methods teachers may rely on. Our data, then, were first treated as a collective case study (Creswell 1998) and then as independent case studies.

Group Findings: DORF and Rates of Reading Literature

DIBELS (Sixth Edition) provides benchmarks for readers in kindergarten through third grade. Since our readers were at the end of second grade, we used the end of second grade benchmarks. The benchmarks provide a range of WCPM matched with identified levels of risk as well as instructional recommendations:

DORF<70   At Risk   Instructional Recommendation:
                                Intensive
70<=DORF<90   Some Risk   Instructional Recommendation:
                                Strategic
DORF>=90   Low Risk   Instructional Recommendation:
                                Benchmark

The first objective of this part of our study was to investigate the relationship between WCPM during reading of authentic text and DORF. Comparing scores for each reader across all reading events, we found that the range of differences for individual readers reading different texts was vast. The two readers who showed the least variation in rates both had a difference of 15 WCPM across the texts they read, and the student who had the greatest variation had a difference of 76 WCPM across texts. For the data set as a whole, the average difference in rate across different texts was 41.54 WCPM. No predictive pattern emerged in regards to text difficulty, number of texts read, the student's retelling proficiency, or any other meaning variables coded in the miscue analysis to explain these variations in rate.

DIBELS assessment is used not only to group students, but also to determine the instruction the students will receive as a result of their DORF scores. The procedure for DORF includes taking three reading rate measures, but then recording only the middle score as that student's rate. Since we had rate and accuracy scores of two to three stories and one recorded DORF for each participant in our study, we were able to see if all reading rates for any single reader would result in the same instructional decision for that student according to DIBELS benchmarks. We found that in ten of the thirteen cases, the students fell into different risk categories depending on what text they read. Expectedly, with a mean variation of 41.54 words, four of these ten readers fell into all of the risk categories. The remaining readers fell into two of the three risk categories. We will include a discussion of instructional recommendations based on DIBELS benchmarks in the cases below.

It was not possible for us to draw any statistical generalizations about these readers from examining their DORF scores in relationship to their reading rates for the literature. However, we can report our observation that eleven of the thirteen readers read the DORF at higher rates than any of the books they read; two students read one text at the same rate but varied drastically while reading another text; and one reader read one text with a high rate of accuracy, yet read another slowly, haltingly. Each of these observations is particular to individual students, and we could find no direct connection to DORF to explain any of these differences. Two students even had almost identical DORF scores (113 and 114) but shared no other similarities in their reading of the trade books.

One pattern did emerge. Remember, these students were grouped for instruction first across the grade level, and again within the classroom. The second grade classroom assignments made at the start of the school year were based on grouping together children who had similar DIBELS assessment scores at the end of first grade. The group of students in the classroom in this study was the highest scoring group of second grade readers in the school. The grouping within the classroom was assigned by the classroom teacher, but again it was based on the students' DIBELS scores—the last shift being made after the midyear assessment. At the end of the year, when this data was collected, we found that the students in the low group did indeed score lower on their DIBELS assessment with the exception of one student whose parent did not give permission for her to participate in the study of literature reading.

Among the readers in our study, however, the DORF scores in the high group (nine students) varied more than the DORF scores in the low group (four students). In other words, there was a greater range of

DORF scores for the students who had met the benchmark of 90 WCPM. The students in the high group also had more variation within reading events than the students in the low group. In fact, some readers' DORF scores were so different than any of their literature reading it led us to wonder how the students could possibly be the same readers. For example, two students sped through the DORF assessment at rates of 114 and 101, but their fastest rate of reading for any of the three literature stories were only 74 and 66 WCPM respectively.

While the higher scoring DORF readers had more variation in reading rates between reading events, the slower readers didn't have such extreme rate differences when they read different texts. The rate variation in the high group was 48 WCPM; the variation in the low group was 27 WCPM. The group sizes and the uneven number of readers in each group did not allow us to claim any statistical generalizations based on this finding. With thirteen students in this part of our study, our goal was not to complete a statistical analysis but to examine the detailed profiles of readers and to ask what DIBELS data can tell us about individual readers.

It is important to note that no sophisticated machines were used to measure these readers' oral reading expression. Because we are trying to determine how useful DIBELS data is to classroom teachers, beyond exact timing of words per minute we relied on careful listening and did not use equipment sometimes used in oral reading research studies that would not be available to classroom teachers.

Reading Rates for Individual Readers

Although each reader in our study had a range of reading rates, as noted above, each reader tells a different story. To illustrate the individuality of readers, we now share the profiles of four readers, two from the high group and two from the low group.

Andy

Andy, from the high instructional group, was the overall fastest reader in the study. He sped through not only his DORF, but also *Cherries*, recording scores of 153 and 141 respectively. His rates for reading *Flossie* (94 WCPM) and *Precious* (105 WCPM) were both above the DIBELS benchmark; according to DIBELS assessment, Andy was at Low Risk (the most proficient of all risk categories), a reader who had reached benchmark and should receive grade level instruction. The rate and accuracy of all three of his literature reading events also landed him in this instructional range. But what did his reading sound like? Did he sound like he was making sense of the reading? Was he able to retell what he read with any level of accuracy?

When listening to Andy read and thinking beyond rate and accuracy, we found that each of Andy's audiotaped reading events sounded different. At times during his reading of *Precious*, Andy read haltingly, almost word-by-word, suggesting that he may indeed have been struggling to comprehend what he was reading. At other times, however, he was able to read in phrases, using intonation that gave the impression he was comprehending the story. His retelling score of 29 percent really came as no surprise after listening carefully to his oral reading—he seemed to understand only parts of the story as he read.

While reading *Flossie*, however, Andy sounded like a very proficient reader. He did not seem to be speeding through the reading, but he read quickly and with a seemingly high degree of accuracy; he paused at punctuation, read in appropriate phrases, and used stress and intonation in ways that indicated he was comprehending as he read. Therefore, his retelling score of 14 percent came as quite a surprise—listening to his reading as teachers we would have expected a much higher level of comprehension.

And what about his third reading event of *Cherries and Cherry Pits*? This is the only story that Andy read in a way that could be characterized as rushed, but this still varied over the course of the story: he rushed through some phrases, read choppy and word-by-word at times, and at other times he read with accurate expression, even chanting sections that were meant to be chanted (for example, "Little lady, little lady" and "Eating cherries and spitting out the pits, eating cherries and spitting out the pits"). These characteristics may leave the listening teacher confused—Andy was reading very quickly, he used expression at times, but at other times his reading was choppy and he didn't slow down to reread or to grasp the expression needed. As the teacher, it might have been best to discuss this reading with Andy as he read or, like Lisa, the teacher quoted in Chapter 1, to say "Whoa, let's reread that," and encourage Andy to slow down. But in a DIBELS classroom speed is good reading and, though Andy scored only 10 percent on his retelling of *Cherries and Cherry Pits*, he was considered a good reader who had reached the benchmark and needed no specific intervention.

Julie

Julie, the second reader from the high group, read the same three books Andy read, but her reading was significantly slower for each reading event. Her average reading rate was 78 WCPM, 44.25 words less than Andy's. In addition, her variation in rate across texts was less than Andy's, only twenty-six words as compared to Andy's sixty. And while Andy's high rates consistently landed him in the lowest risk category for all reading events, only Julie's DIBELS' rate indicated she reached the benchmark. All three of her literature reading events (62, 73, 79) fell short of the target goal of 90 WCPM, and one placed her squarely in the At Risk category—the most concerning, indicating she needed intensive intervention.

But what did we find when we listened more closely to Julie? Interestingly, though Julie seemed to read slowly, her oral renditions led the listener to conclude she was comprehending as she read. That is, her voice rose, fell, sped up, and slowed down as she read. She repeated phrases and sentences, seeming to clarify meaning as she proceeded through each text. And in contrast to Andy, Julie spent time trying to figure out words she didn't immediately recognize. These behaviors indicated that she actively worked to understand each part of the text within the context of the whole story.

For Julie, though her rate fell short of the benchmark goal, her oral reading expression suggested an overall comprehension of the text. But did Julie's retelling scores support this impression of her oral reading? Each of Julie's reading events sounded similar. Her retelling scores did, however, reflect some differences. To begin with, though Julie's rate was much slower than Andy's, her comprehension was much higher (*Precious*, 50 percent; *Flossie*, 57 percent; *Cherries*, 76 percent). And though these were very respectable retelling scores, it is important to determine if there is any indication in the oral reading that Julie was comprehending *Cherries* more completely than either of the other two stories.

Upon further examination, we found nothing to explain the relationship between Julie's speed of reading and her variation in retelling. She read *Cherries* the fastest (79 WCPM) and with the highest comprehension (76 percent), however, her slowest reading did not result in the lowest comprehension. Furthermore, upon careful listening, there was no significant difference in her oral reading characteristics while reading the different stories. And though Julie fell into DIBELS's highest risk category based on rate and accuracy for one of her reading events, a complete profile of her as a reader indicated that she was not a struggling reader.

Daniel

Of the four low readers in this group of thirteen, Daniel showed more variation in his reading than the other three low readers, but not as much variation as Andy. Daniel's three reading events are the DORF assessment and two literature books: *Charles* and *Amy*. We decided to share Daniel's reading because it tells a very different story than any of the other readers in this group, but one that all teachers face at some point in their teaching careers. Daniel was a student who could read but who seemed to dislike reading.

Daniel used expression, took time to figure out words, repeated phrases to correct expression, and even talked to the text while he read. But Daniel also made an occasional loud sigh indicating he was tired of reading, and sometimes yawned with exaggerated loudness giving the impression that reading was bothersome to him. At the same time, he made connecting comments with a somewhat excited voice. For example, while reading the passage in *Amy*, "Walking to the mailbox, Peter looked at the sky. Dark clouds raced across it like wild horses," Daniel quickly commented, "No, it doesn't look like wild horses!" and continued reading. At another time, while reading *Charles*, when Daniel realized Charles cannot see, he excitedly commented, "He needs glasses!"

In spite of these comments that indicate Daniel was connecting to the text, Daniel groaned, sighed, huffed, and dragged through parts of his reading. His reading rate and accuracy was inconsistent, and so were his retelling scores. Daniel's DORF was 85, his WCPM reading *Charles* was 82, and his WCPM reading *Amy* was 45. And though Daniel didn't seem to enjoy reading *Amy*, his retelling score of 50 percent indicated he understood much of the text. On the other hand, his retelling of *Charles* was much lower, just 33 percent, indicating he had less understanding of this text.

Because of the difference in retelling and the obvious attitudinal interference evident during Daniel's reading events, we turned to his miscue data to see if we could find evidence that may explain these differences. The reading profiles for the two stories Daniel read are strikingly similar. He made the same number of miscues per hundred words (5.57 and 5.22) in both stories and used strikingly similar strategies across both texts.

What does this tell us about Daniel? The instructional recommendation for Daniel based on his DIBELS score was that he was at Some Risk and had been targeted for strategic intervention. His rate of reading *Charles* would also result in this recommendation. Daniel read *Amy* at a very slow pace of 45 WCPM, a score that would place him in the highest risk category, yet he has a retelling score of 50 percent for this story.

Do any of these conclusions focus on what we heard while listening to Daniel—that he was really not interested in reading? We don't think so; we believe the first approach to increasing Daniel's reading proficiency would be to get at the heart of his expressed negativity during reading and to work on strategies that increase his motivation to read.

Ethan

Ethan, also in the low group of readers, scored the lowest DORF (68) of all the readers in this study. He was one of the two readers in the group of thirteen whose rates varied the least (15 WCPM), and, like Andy, all of his rate and accuracy scores put him in the same DIBELS' risk category.

Ethan's overall reading rate was slowest of these four readers, averaging 66.66 WCPM. According to DIBELS assessment, Ethan was At Risk needing intensive intervention. DIBELS does not and cannot tell us what this intervention should look like or what Ethan's specific needs were—but what does a close look at authentic reading tell us about Ethan?

To begin with, Ethan's retelling scores mirrored Daniel's; his retelling score for *Charles* was 50 percent but only 33 percent for *Amy*. And like Daniel, Ethan read both books with expression and at times with appropriate speed. Unlike Daniel, however, a teacher listening to

Ethan read might consider Ethan's substitutions a cause for concern. For example, at one point while reading *Amy*, Ethan read:

> Peter started to, Peter started at a sheet of paper for a while and he we-e-el-l this way it's short of special (read with no recognition of new sentence at *we-e-el-l*, but correct end of sentence rising intonation in the word *special*)

rather than

> Peter stared at the sheet of paper for a while and said, "We-e-el-l, this way it's sort of special."

Carefully listening to his oral reading yielded very little about his understanding of the text and only indicated that Ethan could read with sentence level expression while omitting words and substituting words that are semantically incorrect. Because Ethan was making noticeably unacceptable substitutions and yet still read with expression, his reading begged for a careful miscue analysis.

Unlike Daniel, Ethan's reading of the two books showed quite different profiles. While reading *Amy*, Ethan relied more heavily on graphophonic cues than he did while reading *Charles* (74 and 62 respectively). Also important to note was that Ethan used syntactic and semantic cues much less often than he did graphophonics for both stories. When Ethan relied less on graphophonic cues, his retelling score was much higher and resulted in an acceptable retelling score.

It seems that Ethan had few strategies beyond graphophonics to use when reading unfamiliar texts or when texts became too difficult. His overreliance on decoding, at the expense of syntax and semantics, quite possibly interfered with comprehension. With this information, Ethan's teacher could plan strategic lessons that were specific to his needs and not just lump him in an instructional group based on a single rate and accuracy score. Unfortunately, regardless of what reading event rate and accuracy score you use, Ethan would be labeled At Risk and would be tested weekly, much like Joe in this chapter's opening vignette.

Unfortunately, Ethan's weekly assessment of reading rate would emphasize continued reliance on graphophonics and not the importance of making sense while reading and using correction strategies that would increase his understanding of texts. Our data, however, showed that Ethan would benefit most from instruction that focused on meaning and taught him to use other cueing systems (syntactic and semantic) to process the words in the texts he read.

Looking closely at the profiles of these four readers, it is easy to see the extremely limited value of DORF. Even for the two students who fell into the same instructional groups while reading literature, the recommendations of "meets benchmark" and "intensive intervention" provide nothing of value to a teacher making instructional decisions for these students. But careful examination of the entire profile of reading does give valuable information to these students' teacher as discussed in each of the cases above. While we presented only four cases here that illustrate four different readers, similar information can be gleaned from each of the thirteen readers in this study.

Conclusions

We find that relying on a single measure of reading rate and accuracy is misleading. The variation in WCPM measures within our cases leads us to conclude that DIBELS' practice of collecting three scores and discarding two, recording only the middle score should be discontinued. How can one reading event be an accurate representation of a child's overall reading proficiency when such differences are found in so many of our readers? Rather than discarding the students' rate and accuracy scores, we invite teachers and researchers to closely investigate why there is a variation in scores. What can we learn about text differences, motivation, and prior knowledge by examining these vast ranges in reading rates?

Furthermore, we, like Goodman (2006) and Pressley (2006), are concerned that numerous students whose teachers use DIBELS to make placement decisions are being misguided and may be making very different decisions for their students than they may otherwise make. For us, Andy does need specific, targeted instruction as does every one of our students regardless of how proficiently they may or may not be performing. That is our job as teachers—to know specific details about our students' reading performance and to support their development to read ever more complex texts. DIBELS sets a very dangerous precedence of focusing teachers' instructional emphasis on remediation of simplistic features of rate and accuracy rather than on individualizing instruction needed to advance proficiency in the very complex process of reading.

Returning to the original question that framed this study, Are the time and money invested in DIBELS useful for classroom teachers? Our answer is a resounding no. Based upon our study of DIBELS we caution teachers, testers, and parents against accepting any single measure of reading performance, especially DIBELS, as a valid representation of a child's reading proficiency. No simplistic score, especially one that seems as arbitrary as the DORF, can tell us what we need to know about a child's reading.

Should Fluency Be Considered a Critical Component of Reading?

Throughout the chapters in Part II of this book, we presented the findings of our study, drawing implications for fluency theory, instruction, and assessment. In these concluding chapters, we will use what we have learned, to reread common assumptions regarding the role of rate and accuracy in the reading process and current practices that encourage students to read faster and more accurately. Finally, we will ask the question, "If not fluency, then what?" in an effort to forge a new path in conceptualizing the reading process based upon our own findings and those of other researchers.

We began our study with the overall goal of providing teachers with more stable ground upon which they can decide just how much emphasis should be placed on fluency in planning their reading instruction and evaluating their students. To accomplish this, we felt it necessary to adopt the definition of fluency for our study that is currently being operationalized in programs and assessments mandated in response to No Child Left Behind's Reading First. Despite hotly contested theories and definitions of fluency within the academic world, few could deny that the definition of fluency being operationalized in our nation's classrooms is that of rate and accuracy. We therefore examined the roles and relationships of rate and accuracy in the reading process through the use of the gold standard measure, the number of words correctly read per minute (WCPM). Through our examination of WCPM scores in relationship to miscues, retellings, and standardized phonics scores for over one hundred second graders across various programs, we feel confident that our findings shed much needed light upon the role of rate and accuracy in the reading process.

Let's return to the initial questions that framed our study, so that we may summarize our findings and critically assess key theoretical assumptions underlying the most influential conceptualizations of fluency currently impacting practice.

1. What is the relationship between reading rate and accuracy and use of graphophonics in and out of context?
2. What is the relationship between reading rate and accuracy and meaning construction during reading?
3. What is the relationship between reading rate and accuracy and comprehension of text?
4. What is the relationship of reading rate and accuracy to meaning and comprehension for readers of high and low proficiency?
5. Do currently mandated commercial phonics-based programs develop reading rate and accuracy better than literature-based programs?

In posing these particular questions, we challenge the following claims and assumptions underlying the conceptualization of fluency as rapid, accurate word identification:

- Fluency is acquired through, or is synonymous with, highly skilled phonic decoding.
- Fluency results in, or is prerequisite to, comprehension.
- Fluency is a hallmark of successful reading.
- Fluency is best achieved through intensive, systematic phonics.

Once we have addressed our questions and examined these prevailing assumptions we will assess whether fluency deserves the prominent role it has assumed in the theory and practice of reading. We will consider whether the debate over fluency theory should continue to dominate the discourse on reading, and whether we should instead return our attention to developing a more complex, comprehensive theory of reading proficiency.

What is the relationship between reading rate and accuracy and use of graphophonics in and out of context?

Obviously, we posed this question because underlying so much of the theory and practice of fluency is the assumption that there is a direct relationship between decoding skill and the ability to read accurately and quickly. A strong version of this assumption is grounded in the automaticity model originally established by LaBerge and Samuels (1974) and still highly influential today. It regards fluency as rapid, automatic decoding that frees readers' attention for comprehension (see Chapter 2). In other words, fluency is a critical component of reading that is dependent upon a strong foundation in decoding. While interactive theories of reading may incorporate the use of other cues (such as sentence context or background knowledge) into the achievement of rapid and accurate word identification, phonic decoding is still regarded as paramount to the achievement of fluent reading.

If this assumption were true, we would expect to find evidence that faster, more accurate readers are stronger decoders. Conversely, we would expect less fluent (slower, less accurate) readers to be poorer decoders. Recall that we had two ways to assess decoding: performance on the Woodcock Johnson Psycho-Educational Battery-R (WJPE-R) Word Attack subtest (Woodcock and Bonner Johnson 1990), which reflects decoding in isolation; and the miscue analysis variable of graphic and sound similarity, which reflects the use of graphophonic cues in context. Our findings on the relationship between WCPM and both these variables cannot confirm the hypothesis that decoding is foundational to rapid and accurate reading.

Our findings on the Woodcock Johnson subtest reveal that our more and less fluent readers could not be distinguished on the basis of their isolated phonics scores. Our more fluent readers did have an overall higher average percentile rank on the Woodcock Johnson subtest, but these ranged widely from the 17th to 99th percentile (in relation to the normed second graders). This means our most rapid and accurate readers varied greatly in their ability to decode words out of context. Our least fluent readers had a similarly wide range of performance on the Woodcock Johnson subtest, from a low of the 2nd percentile to the 99th percentile (the highest in our study). Twenty percent of our least fluent readers ranked above the 50th percentile and ten percent of them ranked above the 75th percentile.

When we turned our analysis around to test whether Woodcock Johnson subtest phonics scores could predict fluency, we found that it could not. Students with percentile ranks of seventy-five and greater on the Woodcock Johnson subtest had WCPM scores that ranged from 11 to 144. Only 25 percent of these strong decoders had fluency scores of 90 WCPM or higher, a common fluency benchmark for second graders. Students with the lowest percentile ranks in phonics ranged in fluency from 30 to 104 WCPM.

These finding are clearly inconsistent with the theoretical claim that phonic skill is directly related to reading rate and accuracy, at least on standardized assessments of isolated decoding.

Turning to the miscue analysis findings, we examined whether the use of graphophonic cues during the process of reading was related to our measure of rate and accuracy. Again, we found no evidence to confirm the hypothesis that decoding in context was directly related to reading rate and accuracy. The faster, more accurate readers in our study were virtually indistinguishable from the slower, less accurate readers in terms of their use of graphophonic cues as revealed through their miscues.

These findings cast doubt upon formulations of fluency that view it as either synonymous with or dependent upon a high level of decoding skill. When we look at readers reading authentic literature, we see those who read quickly and accurately who do not demonstrate a high level of expertise in phonic decoding on standardized measures. These same readers do not exhibit any greater use of graphophonic cues while reading. We see excellent decoders on the standardized decoding test who read authentic text much slower and less accurately than the transmission models would predict.

Although there may be some legitimacy to teachers' observations that more proficient readers seem to predict text more rapidly and accurately, this may in fact be attributable to factors other than higher use of graphophonics, such as the use of semantic and syntactic cues or background knowledge. It cannot be assumed that slower, less accurate readers are such because of some deficiency in decoding or incompetence in using graphophonic cues. Slower reading could be due to a myriad of factors, including greater reflection, concern for accurate performance, and insufficient or contradictory background knowledge. In terms of accuracy, years of previous miscue analysis research has taught us that it is the quality rather than the quantity of miscues, and readers' use of multiple cues rather than just graphophonics that are more reliable indicators of proficiency (Goodman 1996).

What is the relationship between reading rate and accuracy and meaning construction during reading?

We posed this question in order to examine the assumption that permeates the "official" literature emanating from the National Reading Panel Report and Reading First and that underlies so many theoretical pronouncements on fluency: rapid and accurate reading frees the reader to focus on meaning. This automaticity perspective of fluency is so pervasive that it is treated as a given that does not require scientific validation. We don't agree.

We decided to examine this assumption by assessing the relationship between meaning construction variables derived from the miscue analysis and WCPM. Additionally, we looked at the relationship between the same meaning construction variables and readers' phonic skills out of context and use of graphophonic cues in context. We believe that our findings from these analyses provide excellent evidence to test the validity of the assumption that fluency, defined as accurate and rapid decoding, is beneficial for meaning construction.

We did not find sufficient evidence to support this pervasive assumption. Although a statistically weak (r=.36) correlation between meaning construction and performance on the standardized phonics test was found on the whole, closer examination revealed a huge range in successful meaning construction for both the higher and lower decoders. Meaning construction scores (the percentage of miscues that resulted in NO LOSS of meaning) for the stronger decoders ranged anywhere from 8 to 84 percent. Meaning construction ranged greatly for the weaker decoders as well, from 4 to 85 percent. Looking at the use of graphophonics in the context of reading, we actually found possible counterevidence to the automaticity hypothesis. Students with greater meaning construction during reading actually had a tendency (weak, significant correlations) to use graphophonic cues less than students with weaker meaning construction.

Turning to findings regarding the relationship between reading fluency and meaning construction, we can provide no additional substantiation for the automaticity claim that faster, more accurate reading facilitates or benefits meaning construction. We found no significant correlation between students' rate and accuracy of reading authentic text and either their use of semantic cues or self-correction strategies, indicators of meaningful prediction and monitoring of reading. A weak, positive correlation found between WCPM and NO LOSS of meaning for the readers in the literature-based program reflects a tendency for these students to read quickly and accurately while constructing meaning. For all of the other groups of students there was no relationship between fluency and meaning construction.

What is the relationship between reading rate and accuracy and comprehension of text?

As previously discussed, we concur with Goodman's (1994) distinction between meaning construction during reading and a reader's overall comprehension. For our study, retellings are used to indicate a student's comprehension of a story after reading. According to both transmission and interactive formulations of fluency, we would expect to see a relationship between fluency and comprehension. While transmission models regard rapid, accurate decoding as the necessary ingredient for comprehension, even interactive models of reading consider smooth, accurate, and expressive oral reading to be indicative or at least suggestive of comprehension (Clay 1991; Fountas and Pinnell 2006). Though their definitions of fluency differ, underlying both perspectives is the assumption that accuracy and rate is predictive of reading comprehension. Though there is a substantial research base that points to a link between fluency and performance on standardized comprehension tests (Shinn et al. 1992; Fuchs et al. 2001), few would claim that such a research base exists to support a link between fluency and comprehension in the reading of authentic texts. As previously noted in Chapter 2, references to the NAEP study (Pinnell et al. 1995) as providing this evidence is misleading. For this study, the data on comprehension was derived not from oral reading, but from silent reading, and fluency was assessed on a subsequent oral reading. This study, therefore, falls short in establishing the oft repeated claim that oral reading fluency is necessary for or reflective of comprehension. Though the NAEP study, in our estimation, is the most authoritative thus far in its description of oral reading fluency as a complex and multifaceted characteristic of oral reading, further research is needed to examine its relationship to comprehension. One of the key goals of our study was to conduct such an examination.

Retelling and WCPM scores for all the students in our study were analyzed to determine whether this presumed relationship of rate and accuracy to comprehension could be confirmed for the reading of authentic texts. We found no statistical correlation between the rate and accuracy with which students read and their overall comprehension as reflected in their retellings. We discovered that this finding held true for all subgroups as well, such as program or identified level. This is a striking and critical finding because so many assessments and instructional programs assume this relationship. As intuitively justified as this assumption may be, our study provides evidence that slower, less accurate reading does not necessarily imply poor comprehension; and conversely, rapid, accurate reading does not necessarily imply good comprehension. Some of the fastest readers in our study had the poorest retellings, seemingly having understood very little of what they read. Other readers who we would have predicted would have poor retellings judging from their slow, laborious reading had surprisingly strong retellings. Perhaps it is we, the listeners, who are more disturbed by disfluent reading than the readers themselves!

What is the relationship of reading rate and accuracy to meaning and comprehension for readers of high and low proficiency?

Underlying the current practice of using rate and accuracy to place and group students is the assumption that fluency is a reliable tool for distinguishing between more and less proficient readers. This is obviously true for assessments such as DIBELS that have been widely implemented throughout the country with the help of Louisa Moats and other Reading First consultants with ties to Sopris West, the publisher of DIBELS. In Chapter 9 we examined the efficacy in using DIBELS to assess readers, based on the data we collected for that. But the underlying assumption still needs to be tested by looking at our large data pool and assessing whether fluency, defined as rate and accuracy, really provides useful, convenient information for distinguishing among readers of varying levels of proficiency.

Based upon our findings summarized thus far, it may come as no surprise that we found no evidence that WCPM can serve as a reliable tool for assessing proficiency in any of our analyses, except for teacher identified levels of high, middle, and low readers. Clearly, teachers do attend to the accuracy and rate of their students' oral reading to either intuitively or deliberately assess readers. We did find statistically significant differences in WCPM scores among teacher identified groups, but only between the high and low groups for the phonics-based programs, and only between the high group and all other readers in the literature-based schools. This means that, at best, rate and accuracy served the teachers only in as much as it distinguished among readers on either end of the spectrum. Most importantly, we found it difficult to distinguish among teacher identified groups in other important ways such as meaning construction and comprehension. This suggests the need to dialogue with teachers about the usefulness of oral reading fluency for grouping students.

To further test the hypothesis that fluency is a critical characteristic for distinguishing levels of proficiency, we looked for significant differences in WCPM scores among readers of the progressively more sophisticated texts we selected for our study. Again, we found that rate and accuracy scores could distinguish among readers on extreme ends of the spectrum. While there were no significant differences in WCPM scores among readers of incrementally more challenging texts, we did find it among readers of the chapter book (level 8) and the easy picture books. As previously noted in Chapter 8, any teacher worth her credentials could distinguish among readers this divergent, and doesn't need to spend valuable time formally assessing them to do so.

Theoretically, our findings offer counterevidence to the assumption that fluency is the critical characteristic of reading capable of differentiating among levels of reading development or proficiency. We question whether fluency should even be afforded the distinction of serving as a "dipstick measure" given that it distinguishes among only the extreme ends of the spectrum, easily accomplished through many other means. We find little value to the theoretical assertion that fluency is a critical component of reading, given that it does not point to any other qualitative differences in the reading of authentic texts.

Do currently mandated commercial phonics-based programs develop reading rate and accuracy better than literature-based programs?

So far, we have offered serious challenges to the theoretical claim that decoding is paramount to achieving either rate and accuracy or comprehension. But even if our findings confirmed the importance of decoding skills, we would still be left with the question of whether systematic, intensive phonics instruction is the key to achieving it. The claim that rapid and accurate decoding could only be achieved through intensive, systematic instruction has possibly had the most powerful impact on reading programs today. Where once there were classroom libraries filled with books of various genres, where children were given time to read and discuss books of their choosing, there are now packaged materials that require children to sound out nonsense words and decodable texts. Is this necessary?

Our findings answer this question with a resounding no. We found that the children in the two phonics-based programs had no significant advantage over the children in the literature-based groups in terms of decoding phonics out of context or using graphophonics cues in context. Furthermore, they were at a significant disadvantage for constructing meaning during reading, and retelling what they read with coherence and depth following reading. Despite strong insistence to the contrary, development of phonic skill and graphophonic competence need not require intensive, systematic instruction. Based upon our findings, this can be learned just as well within the context of meaningful reading. There is, therefore, nothing in the way of evidence from our study to justify the elimination of literature-based instruction and much to recommend it.

If Not Fluency, Then What?

As our research reveals, definitions of fluency in terms of rate and accuracy are too narrow to capture the complexities of readers' transactions with text. Groundbreaking research such as eye movement miscue analysis (EMMA) (Paulson and Freeman 2003) and Flurkey's (1998) technological study of oral reading flow point to an alternative view of proficient reading. This research, in conjunction with our own, supports analyzing reading ability in terms of proficiency—effective and efficient reading—that varies across texts and contexts.

Effective Reading
- self-correcting
- substituting words that make sense
- pausing to think in order to create meaning

Efficient Reading
- not self-correcting when understanding has taken place
- omitting words that are unnecessary to creating meaning
- predicting based on background knowledge and linguistic knowledge

Reading proficiency provides a more useful representation of the process—one that conceptualizes it as an act of comprehending. Understanding readers in terms of proficiency (effectiveness and efficiency) is more beneficial for teachers in meeting the needs of their students.

Current eye movement research adds another perspective for using miscue analysis to assess students' reading. The National Reading Panel (NRP) used earlier eye movement research from the 1970s and 1980s to support their claim that readers fixate on every word in a text. This research showed that readers fixated on content words more often than function words. The NRP used this early eye movement research to explain that fluent readers do not skip these function words, which led the NRP to defend a left to right and top to bottom eye movement progression for skilled reading.

But Paulson and Freeman's current eye movement research shows that reading is a transactive process. Unlike the earlier work, their work found that readers do not fixate on (or necessarily see) every letter or every word during their reading of a text. Paulson and Freeman found that readers actually fixate on between one-half and three-quarters of the words in any given text. This is important because they learned that the area in a reader's vision that is in focus while reading is rather small. To see a word physiologically, according to Paulson and Freeman, it is essential to fixate on it. This important discovery helped them realize that reading cannot be as uncomplicated as merely decoding text. Text would be unintelligible if what readers read is based only on the in-focus data sent to the reader's brain.

> The eyes do not plod along regularly through the text but go where the brain directs them in order to gain more text information. The irregular nature of eye movements can at first glance appear haphazard until a closer look reveals that the pattern is to be found not in uniform fixations and fixation durations, but in the reader's quest for meaning. (Paulson and Freeman 2003, 87)

Also, Paulson and Freeman found that readers look at content words at approximately two times the rate at which they look at function words. Words or phrases that were difficult or confusing to the reader were fixated on longer and fixated on more frequently than other words or phrases. The opposite was also true. When readers encountered no problems with areas of text, they fixated less often and for shorter periods on those sections.

As discussed in Chapter 2, Flurkey (1998) uses the definition "to follow a course" to describe this phenomenon of "speed up and slow down." For him, skilled readers usually do not make miscues that change the meaning of the text; on the other hand, as with unskilled readers, these skilled readers when confronted with unfamiliar text make regressions that slow them down. For the unskilled reader, these regressions are frequently slowing their reading even more. Flurkey combined miscue analysis transcripts with his measurements of readers' speed as the speed changed throughout the reading to understand readers acting in response to text. He discovered that readers read more slowly when their predictions did not hold up based on what they expected to see in the text. In fact, readers sped up and slowed down as they read in response to what they perceived.

The relationship between eye movements and miscues, as Paulson and Freeman's work illustrates, is not causal; but instead, it is an observable aspect of readers making sense from text. Eye movement research illustrates that miscues are not caused by poor decoding, lack of sight words, visually skipping words, or careless, rushed, or sloppy reading. In fact, some miscues may involve longer fixations while readers think about meaning. Often readers even fixate on words they omit. Most importantly, however, Paulson and Freeman demonstrate that miscues are a reflection of a complex transactional process in which

> readers look at the text and read not what they physiologically fixate on, but what they perceive. Readers read what they think they see. Reading is a perceptual act, not simply the direct input of graphic data. (2003, 87)

Paulson and Freeman's eye movement research, as well as Flurkey's research on flow, is further documentation that proficient reading is an efficient process of making meaning.

Our research on fluency, when considered in relation to the studies discussed above, alters what has been the common acceptance of fluency as a critical component of reading. This theoretical perspective, that readers construct meaning from text, is rooted in the constructivist theories of Piaget (1976), Vygotsky (1978), Duckworth (1972), Bruner (1986), and others which hold that children actively construct language and knowledge within mediated contexts. The significance of this theoretical perspective for reading is that children cannot be viewed as empty vessels into which information is poured—nonsense words, phonics rules, sight words. Though there is an abundance of research evidence that supports the constructivist nature of language and literacy, very little of it has filtered into fluency assessments of oral reading.

As our analysis has shown, current fluency assessments, mostly based in behaviorist thinking, can only provide a small sliver of information—and at best dubious information—about a reader. It is assumed in this behaviorist perspective that meaning is embodied within the text and is outside of the child. Textual information is poured into the child through accurate reading and tested through the child's fast recall. Fluency assessments developed by outside agencies—researchers and publishing companies—are based on what they have decided readers need to know and how to test that poured-in knowledge. The reading process of an individual student as observed by a knowledgeable teacher is not part of the equation. Smith (1994) sees this as "fundamentally a dispute over whether teachers can and should be trusted to teach and learners trusted to learn" (302).

We believe in, and our research supports, placing readers at the center of assessment and looking at their learning during real literacy events. We trust readers to be informants when it comes to making decisions on their reading ability. As Taylor (1990) has pointed out, it is impossible to understand the complexity of children's learning in artificially constricted classroom environments using artificial assessments. For her, educators need to provide opportunities for children to engage in problem-solving through activities they have participated in organizing. Literacy for her, and for us, is complex and multidimensional. Only teachers in real classrooms can be trusted to understand the complexity that each child brings to the process of reading and the developmental diversity that must be expected.

With this in mind, we have developed the following Reading Proficiency Descriptors (see Figure 11–1), which account for the complexity and diversity in children's reading. As demonstrated by Flurkey's research on flow and Paulson and Freeman's research on eye movements discussed earlier, miscue analysis is a powerful tool for capturing the complexity in children's reading for both researchers and classroom teachers alike. Therefore, the Reading Proficiency Descriptors we present are based on assessing children using miscue analysis. They are not meant to be all-encompassing nor static in nature. Rather, they represent conceptualizations that are dynamic and evolving. For example, we hope to someday learn whether reading effectiveness develops prior to or simultaneously with reading efficiency when reading is taught as a meaning making process—a topic for future research.

Our Reading Proficiency Descriptors explain reading proficiency in terms of effectiveness and efficiency, but are not meant to be hierarchi-

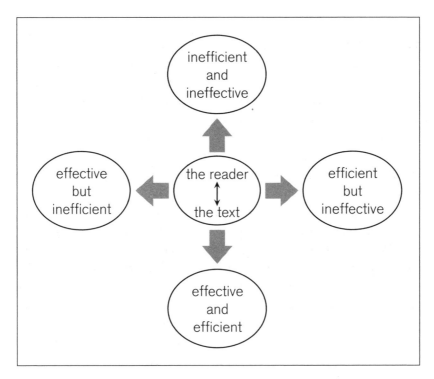

FIGURE 11-1. *Reading Proficiency Descriptors*

cal. Given the findings discussed in Chapter 9, our descriptors needed to allow for variations in an individual student's reading across different texts. In other words, a reader could be effective and efficient on one text, yet effective and inefficient on another depending on the genre or textual characteristics of the particular text. Effective reading indicates that readers use background knowledge, syntax, semantics, text structure, and graphophonics to help self-correct, substitute words, and pause to think in order to construct meaning from text. Comprehending and comprehension are fundamental to effective reading. Efficient reading indicates that readers do not self-correct when understanding has taken place, do omit words that are unnecessary, and do predict based on background and linguistic knowledge. For example, some students in our study read very slowly, stopping on words and self-correcting. Their miscue analysis profiles indicated a high use of syntax and semantics. These students also had high retelling scores. They are effective but inefficient readers. On the other hand, there were efficient but ineffective readers in our study. These readers read accurately and rapidly, yet they did not comprehend the text. Their miscue profiles show that they rarely self-corrected even when their substitutions did not make sense. Some of these readers even substituted nonsense words for real words. For us, proficient readers (effective and efficient), and to a lesser extent effective (but not efficient) readers, are those who use prior textual knowledge to make connections to and transact with current texts; reflect critically about the text being read; and use this knowledge to construct coherent, eloquent, and thoughtful texts in a variety of genres.

It is time that teachers reclaim their classrooms and their students. Assessing students using miscue analysis patterns along with our Reading Proficiency Descriptors will provide teachers with crucial data for planning instruction, for advocating for instructional change, and for discussing reading progress with both parents and administrators. As we have shown, reading instruction must focus on building comprehension. When it does, readers become both more effective and efficient. Through our research, we have come to understand the importance of seeing each reader as unique with his or her own blueprint for creating meaning from text.

Should Fluency
Be Used to Make
Instructional Decisions?

We conducted this research to objectively evaluate the role fluency should have in making instructional decisions. We find ourselves facing similar issues as Shinn and his colleagues were in 1992 when they laid the foundation for their investigation of the role of fluency in comprehension: Given the primary importance of comprehension in the reading process, caution would be indicated when making other decisions about reading skills (e.g., problem identification, problem certification, monitoring of student reading achievement) based only on decoding skills (461).

We have presented evidence throughout this book supporting the position that oral reading fluency, operationalized as rate and accuracy, does not provide an adequate measure of reading ability. In fact, using rate and accuracy alone to assess readers can lead to misguided conclusions that place readers at more risk. This does not mean that rate and accuracy should be ignored, rather it should be seen as part of a larger, complex process. Teachers need to attend to the efficiency and effectiveness of a reader. When a child is reading too slowly to be effective, or focusing on word-by-word reading so much that they are not focusing on meaning, strategy instruction should address this. We do not want to ignore slow and laborious reading; we want to understand it.

What We Learned from Our Research

What follows are key points that are helpful in planning reading instruction and assessment that is complementary to a child's overall reading development.

Caution: Don't Overemphasize the Role of Decoding

The findings from our study clearly indicate we should be very cautious about using students' performance on isolated phonics tasks as indicators of reading proficiency. In fact our study shows that students can be seriously misjudged on the basis of performance on isolated phonics tasks. We would similarly caution against judging students' proficiency on the basis of their use of graphophonics during reading given that it says little about their ability to construct meaning and comprehend what they read.

Overemphasizing the role of decoding at the expense of comprehension in early literacy programs is indeed a very dangerous practice. Curricula based upon models of reading that presuppose meaning can wait until after a series of skills are learned runs the risk of reducing reading to meaningless word calling. As we have seen in our study, when decoding takes instructional precedence over comprehension, students are often required to give a great deal of attention to decoding when they don't need to. Our data indicate that this mega focus on decoding provides no advantage in the development of graphophonic understanding, and yet can run the risk of interfering with students' perception of reading as a meaning constructing process. We believe that children easily master their language; they know how to play with words, to manipulate phonemes, to make rhymes and chants quite naturally. Can't children learn literacy without needing to articulate knowledge about the structure of their language? Isn't it enough for them to simply *do* language (Lindfors 1991), becoming strong readers and writers by reading and writing meaningful texts with the mediation of knowledgeable teachers using strategic instruction?

Our findings show that some readers rely very heavily on graphophonic cues at the expense of reading for meaning. We found a distinct difference in the cues readers used in phonics-based versus literature-based instructional programs. We cannot help but wonder if the current heavy focus on phonic skills at the expense of comprehension in formal instruction is forcing young readers' natural curiosity and playfulness out of the reading process, resulting in a redefinition of reading as mouthing words quickly and accurately. Is the current focus on rate and accuracy going to help readers develop as thoughtful, lifelong readers? Or will the intense attention currently being given to speed send the wrong message, resulting in the kind of readers Lisa Jacobs described in Chapter 1—readers who think good reading is fast reading rather than meaningful reading?

Our research confirms that teaching reading as a word-by-word process creates readers who read one word at a time, focusing on words instead of meaning. Students need to use meaning and language sense to construct meaning. Young readers need to learn a variety of strategies and not focus on simply reading faster. The idea that a good reader is a fast reader may actually be detrimental to developing comprehension strategies. Teaching students to speed through reading does not help them learn to make sense of text, to think while they read, or to combine multiple cueing systems to understand text.

Nonsense Words Are Nonsensical

Grouping readers based on rate and accuracy is founded on Curriculum Based Measurement (CBM) research. The only link to comprehension that CBM provides is standardized testing comprehension results, which in and of themselves are of limited value in making daily instructional decisions. Ironically, DIBELS and other popular commercial assessment programs that use CBM procedures are not even curriculum-based measurements. To qualify as a curriculum-based measurement an assessment would need to be based upon all or part of the instructional materials used to teach the assessed student.

We are particularly concerned about the practice of reading nonsense words in early literacy classrooms that is being fueled by concerns over fluency assessments. Our preservice teachers are in first grade classrooms where nonsense word walls have become the norm and where teachers include nonsense word reading in their instructional lessons. These are well-intentioned teachers who believe it is only fair to teach their students what they will face in an assessment, especially an assessment that can potentially label a child as a high risk reader.

Experimental researchers intentionally decontextualized phonics instruction and assessment, moving it as far from meaning-based reading as possible, in order to more purely measure specific treatment effects on the development of phonic knowledge. Decontextualized phonics tasks, such as the reading of pseudo words, has moved from experimental research methods to assessment programs and from assessment programs to instruction. But we believe this practice, which may or may not be valid for research, is unethical and counterproductive for teaching and learning. We contend that the goals of researchers can be very different from the goals of teachers, and that moving experimental designs into our classrooms for wholesale practice on young readers is misguided and potentially harmful.

Put Meaning First

Oral fluency benchmark goals have become an all too common tool used to place and level students. As Pressley (2006) notes, assessing readers for instructional purposes cannot be as simple as taking a quick dipstick measure. Pressley and colleagues found that DIBELS oral reading assessments only predicted 20 percent of the variance on a more comprehensive reading test when given at the third grade level. After conducting our research we are not at all surprised by Pressley's findings. Our findings indicate that we cannot assume a reader has just one fluency rate—in fact we found that a single reader's rate and accuracy varies across multiple texts. Using one simplistic measure of reading success cannot possibly provide a comprehensive description of a reader.

It is assumed that students who read quickly and accurately comprehend what they read. But do they? Acting on conclusions drawn from a partial view of a reader leads to incorrect placement decisions and potentially harmful instruction. Our findings indicate that teachers are indeed grouping students and making instructional decisions for students based on measures of fluency, but that these measures do not correlate with the students' ability to comprehend what they read. Students who read faster were consistently identified as good readers and students who read more slowly were in the low group. But a complete picture of these students revealed that the fast, good readers did not consistently have high comprehending and comprehension scores. Conversely, the slow readers were not necessarily low comprehenders. Many readers were inaccurately labeled using this crude measure of rate and accuracy, thus indicating this method of evaluation should not be used for instructional grouping. Rate and accuracy do not distinguish between high and low readers except at extreme ends of the spectrum and leave many students mislabeled. Given these findings, the current practice of basing instructional decisions on a student's rate and accuracy should be discontinued immediately.

What Should We Teach?

As a result of the Reading First section of No Child Left Behind, teachers face mandates that force them to execute skill-based phonics programs and scripted assessments in their classrooms. Teachers are no longer able to act using their knowledge of the teaching and learning process to evaluate what individual instructional approach each student needs in order to advance her literacy development. Like Rasinski and Padak (2004), we view literacy development as a multifaceted, complex process that has no simple curriculum guide that will meet the needs of all students. Serious consideration should be given to instructional time, text difficulty, genres of texts, attention to reading, writing, and oral language, as well as the increasingly neglected responsibility teachers have in helping students develop a desire to read.

Meaning-centered Approach

Young readers need a meaning-centered approach to reading instruction. Based on our findings, literature-based meaning-centered reading provides children with just as much ability to use graphophonics as an intensive phonics approach. A meaning-centered approach keeps the reader focused on the ultimate goal of reading—comprehension. In our work with teachers, we have found that some current instructional practices touted as tried and true ways to increase fluency have their foundation in meaning-based, whole language instruction. Repeated reading, shared reading, choral reading, independent reading, and readers' theater are currently being implemented for the sole purpose of improving fluency. These practices were developed to help readers focus on meaning. Having been hijacked by a fluency first campaign, however, their affect on learning is quite different. When students know the goal of a lesson is to increase speed, speed is what they focus on. Similarly, when they know meaning is the focus of a lesson, meaning is what they work to improve. We must keep meaning at the center of instruction; creating fluent readers without considering comprehension as the primary goal of reading is irresponsible practice.

Provide Flexible Grouping That Attends to Individual Profiles of Readers

We know from Allington's work (2006) that "teachers typically interact differently with students who differ in reading proficiency. They not only interact differently, but they also organize lessons differently" (96). The implications of this knowledge coupled with current grouping strategies based on fluency assessments are particularly problematic. Lumping students together to increase their oral reading proficiency without assessing their complete reading profiles will inevitably lead to poor instruction.

There are numerous reasons a reader may read a passage at a given rate. No assessor can listen to a reader read aloud for one minute and make a valid determination of why that reader is slowing or speeding up in his reading. Readers who are making connections to the reading may slow down to savor the moment—to simply enjoy reading for the moment or to remember another text or time in their lives when they felt like the character. Readers may also slow down to think about a particular word or passage in an effort to keep the image in their minds before moving on. Readers may also slow down because they do not understand a particular word or point being made in the reading. On the other hand, readers who are bored with a particular passage may speed up and skip words or phrases in an effort to get to a point where the reading interests them. Readers who are not connecting, whose minds are elsewhere, may move very quickly through a passage, only to get to a point well into the reading and realize they really do not know what they just read. A complete profile of a reader can help an assessor determine why a reader reads at a given pace.

A complete miscue profile of a reader also provides information on the use of graphophonic, syntactic, and semantic cues, as well as predicting, confirming and correcting strategies. A teacher can use this to plan appropriate instructional approaches that will support the development of that reader and others with similar profiles. If a reader continuously struggles to predict words that fit grammatically in a sentence, are canned lessons in vowel digraphs going to help? If a reader reads quickly and accurately but with little or no comprehension, should that student be grouped with a student who reads at a similar pace, with similar accuracy, but with high levels of understanding?

Students need strategies to continue reading when they come upon a word they do not know or a passage they do not understand. Explicit instruction in all aspects of reading is necessary, but determining who gets what instruction is a complex decision-making process that cannot be reduced to simply checking a reader's rate and accuracy. Explicit instruction should be part of supporting a learner's reading development, but this instruction should be planned and executed based on the individual reader's reading proficiency and needs. We cannot just group students as "above, at, and below grade level" to plan high quality reading instruction.

Variety in Reading Tasks

Students need "appropriately difficult texts," which Allington has called for on numerous occasions since 1977. His point is very clear: readers need to be matched with texts they can read. We agree and would like to bring another dimension to this conversation: readers read different texts very differently and readers' levels of proficiency cannot be determined by reading a single text. We need to provide early reading instruction using a variety of texts and genres. In our study, no reader's profile remained unchanged from text to text—in fact, quite the opposite was true. Even though the genre of text the students read did not change, their interactions with the texts did. Rates of reading varied as well as comprehending and comprehension indicators. Reading instruction must take into account the text a student reads as well as the tasks associated with reading.

Students must be afforded instructional opportunities and programs that do not rush them through a series of tasks, but rather help them to understand that the rate of reading should be appropriate to the genre and purpose of reading.

As educators, it is our responsibility to provide authentic and valuable learning opportunities for our students. To do so, we need to understand their strengths as well as their needs and help them to become critical readers. We cannot do this by following dogmatic practices steeped in political ideology. Instead, we need to reclaim our roles as professionals who listen to the voices of each and every reader and let them lead the way.

References

Allington, Richard. 2006. "Fluency: Still Waiting After All of These Years." In *What Research Has to Say About Fluency Instruction*, edited by Alan Farstrup and Jay Samuels, 94–105. Newark, DE: International Reading Association.

———. 2002. *Big Brother and the National Reading Panel: How Ideology Trumped Evidence*. Portsmouth, NH: Heinemann.

———. 1983. "Fluency: The Neglected Reading Goal in Reading Instruction." *Reading Teacher* 36: 556–61.

Altwerger, Bess, ed. 2005. *Reading for Profit: The Commercialization of Reading Instruction*. Portsmouth, NH: Heinemann.

Altwerger, Bess, Poonam Arya, Lijin Jin, Barbara Later, Prisca Martens, G. Patricia Wilson, and Nancy Wiltz. 2004. "When Research and Mandates Collide: The Challenges and Dilemmas of Teacher Education in the Era of NCLB." *English Education* 36: 119–33.

Armbruster, Bonnie, and Jean Osborn. 2001, 2003. *Put Reading First*. Washington, DC: Partnership for Reading.

Barone, Diane, Darrin Hardman, and Joan Taylor. 2006. *Reading First in the Classroom*. Boston: Pearson Education.

Bascia, N., and A. Hargreaves. 2000. *The Sharp Edge of Educational Change: Teaching, Leading and the Realities of Reform*. New York, New York: Routledge Falmer.

Blachowicz, Camille, Mary Kay Moskal, Jennifer Massarelli, Connie Obrochta, Ellen Fogelberg, and Peter Fisher. 2006. "Everybody Reads: Fluency as a Focus for Staff Development." In *Fluency Instruction: Research-Based Best Practices*, edited by Timothy Rasinski, Camille Blachowicz, and Kristen Lems, 141–54. New York: Guilford Press.

Bruner, Jerome. 1986. *Actual Minds, Possible Worlds*. Cambridge, MA: Harvard University Press.

Carnine, Douglas, Jerry Silbert, and Edward Kameenui. 1997. *Direct Instruction in Reading*, 3d ed. Upper Saddle River, NJ: Merrill.

Clay, Marie. 1991. *Becoming Literate: The Construction of Inner Control*. Portsmouth, NH: Heinemann.

Cohen, Barbara, and Daniel Mark Duffy. 1990. *Molly's Pilgrim*. New York: Yearling.

Cohen, Miriam. 1997. *See You Tomorrow, Charles*. New York: Yearling.

Coles, Gerald. 2003. *Reading the Naked Truth: Literacy, Legislation, and Lies.* Portsmouth, NH: Heinemann.

Committee of Fifteen on Elementary Education. 1895. *Report of the Committee on Elementary Education with the Reports of the Subcommittees: On the Training of Teachers; On the Correlation of Studies in Elementary Education; On the Organization of City School Systems.* Washington, DC: National Education Association (report of the sub-committee on the correlation of studies in elementary education, p. 40–99).

Creswell, John. 1998. *Qualitative Inquiry and Research Design: Choosing Among Five Traditions.* Thousand Oaks, CA: Sage.

Dowhower, Sarah. 1987. "Effects of Repeated Reading on Second-Grade Transitional Readers' Fluency and Comprehension." *Reading Research Quarterly* 22 (4): 390–406.

Duckworth, Eleanor. 1972. *"The Having of Wonderful Ideas" and Other Essays on Teaching and Learning.* New York: Columbia University Press.

Ehri, Linnea. 1998. "Grapheme-Phoneme Knowledge is Essential for Learning to Read Words in English." In *Word Recognition in Beginning Literacy*, edited by Jamie L. Metsala and Linnea C. Ehri, 3–40. Mahwah, NJ: Lawrence Erlbaum.

Engelmann, Siegfried, and Susan Hanner. 1995. *Reading Mastery IV Presentation Book.* Worthington, OH: SRA.

Flurkey, Alan. 1998. "Reading as Flow: A Linguistic Alternative to Fluency." In *Occasional Papers*, edited by Kenneth Goodman and Yetta Goodman. Tucson, AZ: University of Arizona, College of Education Program in Language and Literacy.

Ford, Michael. 2001. "What to Do About Jabbering Parrots: Lessons Learned While Advocating Best Practices." *Language Arts* 79: 53–60.

Fountas, Irene, and Gay Su Pinnell. 2006. *Teaching for Comprehending and Fluency: K–8.* Portsmouth, NH: Heinemann.

———. 2000. *Leveled Books for Readers.* Portsmouth, NH: Heinemann.

———. 1996. *Guided Reading: Good First Teaching for All Children.* Portsmouth, NH: Heinemann.

Fuchs, Lynn S., and Douglas Fuchs. 1999. "Monitoring Student Progress Toward the Development of Reading Competence: A Review of Three Forms of Classroom-Based Assessment." *School Psychology Review* 28 (4): 659–671.

Fuchs, Lynn S., Douglas Fuchs, Michelle Hosp, and Joseph Jenkins. 2001. "Oral Reading Fluency as an Indicator of Reading Competence: A Theoretical, Empirical, and Historical Analysis." *Scientific Studies of Reading* 5 (3): 239–56.

Garan, Eileen. 2001. *Resisting Reading Mandates: How to Triumph with the Truth.* Portsmouth, NH: Heinemann.

Giroux, Henry. 1992. *Border Crossings: Cultural Workers and the Politics of Education*. New York: Routledge, Chapman, and Hall.

Good, Roland, and Ruth Kaminski. 2002. *Dynamic Indicators of Basic Early Literacy Skills*, 6th ed. Eugene, OR: Institute for the Development of Educational Achievement.

Goodman, Kenneth. 2006. *The Truth About DIBELS: What It Is—What It Does*. Portsmouth, NH: Heinemann.

———. 2004. "Reading, Writing and Written Texts: A Transactional Sociopsycholinguistic View." In *Theoretical Models and Processes of Reading*, 5th ed., edited by Robert B. Ruddell and Norman J. Unrau. Newark, DE: International Reading Association.

———. 2003. "Reading, Writing, and Written Texts: A Transactional Sociopsycholinguistic View." In *On the Revolution of Reading: The Selected Writings of Kenneth S. Goodman*, edited by Alan Flurkey and Jingguo Xu. Portsmouth, NH: Heinemann.

———. 1996. *On Reading*. Toronto: Scholastic.

———. 1982. Language and Literacy: *The Selected Writings of Kenneth S. Goodman*, (ed. with Frederick Gollasch). Boston: Routledge and Kegan Paul.

———. 1967. "Word Perception: Linguistic Bases." *Education*, Vol. 87, May 1967, pp. 539–543.

Goodman, Yetta, Dorothy Watson, and Carolyn Burke. 2005. *Reading Miscue Inventory: From Evaluation to Instruction*, 2nd ed. Katonah, NY: Richard Owen.

———. 1987. *Reading Miscue Inventory: Alternative Procedures*. Katonah, NY: Richard Owen.

Graves, Donald. 2003. *Writing: Teachers and Children at Work*. Portsmouth, NH: Heinemann.

———. 2001. *Testing Is* Not *Teaching: What Should Count in Education*. Portsmouth, NH: Heinemann.

Hasbrouck, Jan, and Gerald Tindal. 2006. "Oral Reading Fluency Norms: A Valuable Assessment Tool for Reading Teachers." *Reading Teacher* 59: 636–43.

———. 1992. "Curriculum-Based Oral Reading Fluency Norms for Students in Grades Two Through Five." *Teaching Exceptional Children* 24 (3): 41–44.

Hutchins, Pat. 1978. *Happy Birthday, Sam*. New York: Harper Collins.

Johnston, Susan. 2006. "The Fluency Assessment System: Improving Oral Reading Fluency with Technology." In *Fluency Instruction: Research-Based Best Practices*, edited by Timothy Rasinski, Camille Blachowicz, and Kristen Lems, 123–40. New York: Guilford Press.

Jordan, Nancy. 2005. "Basal Readers and Reading as Socialization: What Are Children Learning?" *Language Arts* 82 (3): 204–13.

Keats, Ezra Jack. 1998. *A Letter to Amy.* New York: Puffin.

Keats, Ezra Jack. 1967. *Peter's Chair.* New York: Harper & Row.

Krashen, Steven D. 2001. "More Smoke and Mirrors: A Critique of the National Reading Panel Report on 'Fluency.'" *Phi Delta Kappan* 83 (2): 118–21.

LaBerge, David, and S. Jay Samuels. 1974. "Toward a Theory of Automatic Information Processing in Reading." *Cognitive Psychology* 6: 293–323.

Lindblom, Charles, and Edward Woodhouse. 1993. *The Policy-Making Process.* Englewood Cliffs, NJ: Prentice-Hall.

Lindfors, Judith. 1991. *Children's Language and Learning.* Needham Heights, MA: Allyn and Bacon.

Martens, Prisca, Poonam Arya, Pat Wilson, and Lijin Jin. 2005, December 2. *The Impact of Text Characteristics on Second Graders' Readings and Retellings of Texts with Contrasting Story Structures.* National Reading Conference Annual Meeting, Miami, FL.

McKissack, Patricia. 2005. *Precious and the Boo Hag.* New York: Atheneum/Anne Schwartz Books.

———. 1992. *Flossie and the Fox.* New York: Scholastic Inc.

Merriam, Sharon. 1990. *Case Study Research in Education: A Qualitative Approach.* San Francisco: Jossey-Bass.

National Institute of Child Health and Human Development. 1992a. *Report of the National Reading Panel: Teaching Children to Read: Reports of the Subgroups.* Washington, DC: NICHD.

———. 1992b. *Reports of the National Reading Panel: Teaching Children to Read: Summary.* Washington, DC: NICHD.

Paulson, Eric, and Ann Freeman. 2003. *Insight from the Eyes: The Science of Effective Reading Instruction.* Portsmouth, NH: Heinemann.

Piaget, Jean. 1976. *Language and Thought of the Child.* New York: Penguin.

Pikulski, Jay, and David Chard. 2005. "Fluency: Bridge Between Decoding and Reading Comprehension." *Reading Teacher* 58 (6): 510–19.

Pinnell, Guy Su, John Pikulski, Karen Wixson, Jay Campbell, Phillip Gough, and Alexandra Beatty. 1995. *Listening to Children Read Aloud: Oral Fluency.* Washington, DC: National Center for Educational Statistics, U.S. Department of Education.

Poyner, Leslie, and Paula Wolfe, eds. 2005. *Marketing Fear in America's Public Schools: The Real War on Literacy.* Mahwah, NJ: Lawrence Erlbaum Associates.

Pressley, Michael. 2006, April 29. *What the Future of Reading Research Could Be.* Paper presented at the The International Reading Association's Reading Research Conference, Chicago, IL.

———. 1998. *Reading Instruction That Works: The Case for Balanced Teaching.* New York: Guilford Press.

Rasinski, Timothy. 1990. "Investigating Measures of Reading Fluency." *Educational Research Quarterly* 14 (3): 37–44.

Rasinski, Timothy, and Nancy Padak. 2004. "Beyond Consensus-Beyond Balance: Toward a Comprehensive Literacy Curriculum." *Reading and Writing Quarterly* 20: 91–204.

Reutzel, D. Ray. 2006. "Hey, Teacher, When You say 'Fluency,' What Do You Mean?" In *Fluency Instruction: Research-Based Best Practices*, edited by Timothy Rasinski, Camille Blachowicz, and Kristen Lems, 62–85. New York: Guilford Press.

Rosenblatt, L. 1994. *The Reader, the Text, the Poem: The Transactional Theory of the Literary Work*. Carbondale, IL: Southern Illinois University Press.

Samuels, S. Jay. 2006. Reading Hall of Fame Members Discuss and Critique No Child Left Behind. Paper presented at International Reading Association Fifty-First Annual Convention, 2006, May, Chicago, IL

———. 1992. "Toward a Model of Reading Fluency." In *What Research Has to Say About Reading Instruction*, edited by S. Jay Samuels and Alan E. Farstrup. Newark, DE: International Reading Association.

Selden, George. 1960. *The Cricket in Times Square*. New York: Farrar, Strauss and Giroux.

Shanahan, Timothy. 2006. "Developing Fluency in the Context of Effective Literacy Instruction." In *Fluency Instruction: Research-Based Best Practices*, edited by Timothy Rasinski, Camille Blachowicz, and Kristen Lems, 21–38. New York: Guilford Press.

———. 2006. "Does He Really Think Kids Shouldn't Read?" *Reading Today* 23 (6): 12.

Shelton, Nancy R. 2005. "First Do No Harm: Teachers' Reactions to Mandating Reading Mastery." In *Reading for Profit: How the Bottom Line Leaves Kids Behind*, ed. Bess Altwerger. Portsmouth, NH: Heinemann.

Shinn, Mark, Roland Good, Nancy Knutson, W. David Tilly, and Vicki Collins. 1992. "Curriculum-Based Measurement of Oral Reading Fluency: A Confirmatory Analysis of Its Relation to Reading." *School Psychology Review* 21 (3): 459–79.

Short, Kathy, and Carolyn Burke. 1996. "Examining Our Beliefs and Practices Through Inquiry." *Language Arts* 73 (2): 97–104.

Sleeter, Caroline. 1996. *Multicultual Education as Social Activism*. Albany, NY: SUNY Press.

Smith, Frank. 1994. *Understanding Reading*, 5th ed. Hillsdale, NJ: Lawrence Erlbaum Associates.

———. 1986. *Insult to Intelligence*. New York: Arbor House.

Snow, Catherine, Susan Burns, and Peg Griffin, eds. 1998. *Preventing Reading Difficulties in Young Children*. Washington, DC: National Research Council, National Academy Press.

SRA/McGraw-Hill. 2000. Open Court. Desoto, TX: SRA.

Taylor, Denny. 1990. "Teaching Without Testing: Assessing the Complexity of Children's Literacy Learning." *English Education* 22: 4–74.

U.S. Department of Education, Office of Elementary and Secondary Education. 2002. *No Child Left Behind Desk Reference*. Washington, DC. www.ed.gov/admins/lead/account/nclbreference/index.html.

U.S. Department of Education, Office of the Inspector General. 2007. *The Department's Administration of Selected Aspects of the Reading First Program—Final Audit Report*. Publication ED-OIG/A03G0006. Washington, DC: U.S. Government Printing Office.

———. 2006. *The Reading First Program's Grant Application Process—Final Inspection Report*. Publication ED-OIG/13-F0017. Washington, DC: U.S. Government Printing Office.

Vygosky, L. S. 1978. *Mind in Society: The Development of Higher Psychological Processes*, edited by Michael Cole, Vera John-Steiner, Sylvia Scribner, and Ellen Souberman. Cambridge, MA: Harvard University Press.

Williams, Vera. 1991. *Cherries and Cherry Pits*. New York: Harper Trophy.

Wiltz, Nancy, and G. Pat Wilson. 2005. "An Inquiry into Children's Reading in one Urban School Using SRA Reading Mastery (Direct Instruction)." *Journal of Literacy Research* 37 (4): 493–528.

Woodcock, Richard, and M. Bonner Johnson. 1990. *Woodcock Johnson Psycho-Educational Battery-R*. New York: Riverside.

Yatvin, Joan. 2002. "Babes in the Woods: The Wanderings of the National Reading Panel." *Kappan* 83 (5): 364–69.

Index

and decoding, 44–48
DORF measure of, 36, 73–87
and effective reading, 69–72
and efficient reading, 69–70
as fluency measure, 13–15, 26, 27, 34–36, 88
inadequacy of measure, 97, 103
versus meaning, 5, 106
and meaning construction, 92–93
phonics *versus* literature-based programs and, 55–59, 96
and reading proficiency, 63–72, 94–95
and use of graphophonics, 89–91
variation with type and purpose of reading, 42
Reading
fluency as critical component of, 9, 21, 24, 88–96
key areas of, federal identification of, 24
meaning-centered approach in, 107
oral. *See* Fluency; Oral reading
Reading Excellence Act (REA), 4
Reading First, 23–25, 107
commercial programs claiming compliance with, 53
cronyism and corruption in, 3, 24–25
decoding skills under, 50
DIBELS supported by, 74
fluency as pillar in, 9, 24
oral reading emphasis in, 6
Reading First Grant Funding Office, 24–25
Reading fluency. *See* Fluency
Reading Leadership Academies, 25
Reading levels
book levels and, 64, 67–69
DIBELS and, 75, 86–87
flexibility and individual profiles in, 107–109
fluency and, 63–72, 106

identified, comparison of, 64–72
meaning construction and, 64, 65–66
retelling and, 65
teacher identification of, 64
Reading proficiency
as alternative to fluency concept, 97–102
effective reading in, 69–72, 97–102
efficient reading in, 69–70, 97–102
fluency relationship to, 63–72, 94–95
qualitative assessment by teachers, 72
Reading Proficiency Descriptors, 100–102, *101*
Reading tasks, variety in, 109
Reading Today, 6
Reading wars, 3–5
Recoding perspective, 9–13, *10*
"The Report of the Sub-committee on the Correlation of Studies in Elementary Education," 4
Researchers' goals, *versus* teachers' goals, 106
Research methods, 27–36
Retell Fluency, DIBELS, 36, 75, 77
Retelling
comprehension and, 39–41, 94
decoding and, 50–52
DIBELS findings and, 80–86
methods of assessing, 30–31, 36
phonics *versus* literature-based programs and, 56–57
reading levels and, 65
RMC Research Corporation, 25
Running record, 27, 64

Samuels, S. J., 20, 25–26
Scientific movement, 4
See You Tomorrow, Charles (Cohen), 76–77, 81–85